Horatio Rogers

Record of the Rhode Island excursion to Gettysburg

October 11-16, 1886

Horatio Rogers

Record of the Rhode Island excursion to Gettysburg
October 11-16, 1886

ISBN/EAN: 9783744732246

Printed in Europe, USA, Canada, Australia, Japan

Cover: Foto ©ninafisch / pixelio.de

More available books at **www.hansebooks.com**

RECORD

OF THE

RHODE ISLAND EXCURSION

TO

GETTYSBURG,

OCTOBER 11-16, 1886,

WITH THE

DEDICATORY SERVICES OF THE BATTLEFIELD MEMORIALS OF THE SECOND RHODE ISLAND VOLUNTEERS, AND BATTERIES A AND B, FIRST R. I. LIGHT ARTILLERY.

EDITED BY

HORATIO ROGERS,

LATE COLONEL SECOND R. I. VOLS. AND BVT. BRIG. GEN'L U. S. V., CHAIRMAN OF EXCURSION COMMITTEE.

PROVIDENCE, R. I.
E. L. FREEMAN & SON, STATE PRINTERS.
1887.

RECORD

OF THE

RHODE ISLAND EXCURSION

TO

GETTYSBURG,

OCTOBER 11-16, 1886,

WITH THE

DEDICATORY SERVICES OF THE BATTLEFIELD ME-
MORIALS OF THE SECOND RHODE ISLAND
VOLUNTEERS, AND BATTERIES A
AND B, FIRST R. I. LIGHT
ARTILLERY.

EDITED BY

HORATIO ROGERS,

LATE COLONEL SECOND R. I. VOLS. AND BVT. BRIG. GEN'L U. S. V.; CHAIRMAN OF EX-
CURSION COMMITTEE.

PROVIDENCE, R. I.
E. L. FREEMAN & SON, STATE PRINTERS.
1887.

Rhode Island Excursion to Gettysburg,

OCTOBER. 1886.

The following resolution was passed by the General Assembly of Rhode Island, April 14, 1885, viz:

Resolved. That the sum of three thousand dollars is hereby appropriated to perpetuate the participation of the Rhode Island troops at the battle of Gettysburg, to be expended under the supervision of Messrs. Horatio Rogers, Elisha H. Rhodes, Amos M. Bowen, 2nd R. I. Volunteers, D. Coit Taylor and Chas. Cornell, Battery " B." Wm. Millen and Pardon S. Jastram, Battery " E." Benjamin H. Child and James P. Rhodes, Battery " A," in manner following. that is to say: One thousand dollars thereof to be paid to the president and directors of the Gettysburg Battlefield Memorial Association to be expended in the purchase of additional grounds of special interest upon said battlefield, and especially for a site for the memorial of Battery E, First Rhode Island Light Artillery, hereinafter mentioned, and in acquiring rights of way in constructing roads and avenues, in the preservation of natural and artificial defences and in the erection of such memorial structures as are contemplated by the charter of said Association ; also a sum not exceeding five hundred dollars each, to be paid to the 2nd Rhode Island Veteran Association, Battery A. Battery B and Battery E, Veteran Associations of the First Rhode Island Light Artillery, respectively. whenever it shall be shown to said committee that said respective Veteran Associations have caused to be erected on the battlefield of Gettysburg a memorial of their respective regiment or batteries satisfactory to the Superintendent of Tablets and Legends of said Gettysburg Battlefield Memorial Association, but the sums so paid respectively shall not exceed the actual cost of the respective memorials ; and the state auditor is hereby authorized and directed from time to time to draw his orders on the general treasurer for said sums out of any money in the treasury not otherwise appropriated, upon the order of said committee.

The persons named in the resolution were appointed committees by their respective Associations at the reunions held in the summer of 1885, to procure suitable memorials and cause them to be erected on the battlefield of Gettysburg, and before the end of June, 1886, all the memorials had been placed in position ready for dedication. That of the Second Rhode Island Volunteers cost one thousand dollars, the Association having added five hundred dollars to the amount appropriated by the State, while the three batteries limited the cost of their memorials to the amount of the State appropriation. Those of the Second Rhode Island Volunteers and Batteries A and E, were designed and constructed by the Smith Granite Company of Westerly, but that of Battery B was the workmanship of John Flaherty of Niantic.

The memorial of the Second Rhode Island Volunteers is eight feet six inches high, and consists of a square monument of Westerly granite, simple in form, with sharp, well-defined outlines, supporting a bronze group of military devices. The ground base is four and a half feet square and eighteen inches high, with a rough quarried surface, while all the other surfaces are fine hammered. The second base, which is three feet ten inches square and one foot eight inches high, has a deep wash or sloping surface from its upper edge or junction with the die or principal stone. In bold relief on the front of this base is the Sixth Corps badge and this sunken inscription, "July 2 and 3, 1863." The plain massive die, which is two feet ten inches square and three feet eight inches high, is only relieved on its front by a circular sunken disk containing the carved and polished arms of the State of Rhode Island, above which are the words "2nd R. I. Volunteers," and below, "Second Brigade, Third Division, Sixth Corps." Upon the die rests a painted capstone, and the whole is crowned by a group of war devices in bronze, forming the most striking feature of the memorial and representing, in full size, a drum, on which at the right rests a belt, a cartridge box, a bayonet scabbard and a canteen, with a cap on the top, near the front edge of the drum, and a large laurel wreath leaning against it on the left. This memorial is located at the northeasterly base of Little Round Top upon the easterly side of what is now Battle Avenue, and near the entrance of what is now termed Little Round Top Park—it being on or close by the spot where the Second Rhode Island first went into line of battle and where it passed the night of July 2d, 1863.

The memorial of Battery A is also executed in selected Westerly granite, the perpendicular face of the lower base being left rough, while all the rest is finished in fine hammered work. The lower base is four and a half feet square, the second base three and a half feet, the die two feet ten inches at bottom and two feet eight inches at top, the total height, including capstone, being seven feet nine inches. The front of the die is covered with a raised and polished design representing the arms of the State of Rhode Island grouped with a gun, a wheel and crossed sponge staffs, all of about half size. The inscription in sunken letters on the front is " Arnold's Battery, July 2 and 3, 1863 "; on the right, " Battery A, First R. I. L. A., Artillery Brigade, Second Corps "; on the left, " Four Killed, Twenty-four Wounded." The cap stone, which is perpendicular in front and rear, and with a wash showing at the sides, is terminated with a heavy trefoil cresting, the end view or cross section of which, as seen at front and rear, where it slightly projects, forms the outline of the badge of the Second Corps, to which the battery was attached.

The memorial of Battery A is about a hundred yards north of that of Battery B, both being upon Battle Avenue, the former on the west side and the latter on the east. Both memorials stand upon ground occupied by the respective batteries during the third day's fight as well as very near the spots occupied during the second day's fight, and both are close by the angle and the famous clump of little trees which the Confederate Gen. Pickett took as the point of direction in his desperate charge of July 3d.

The memorial of Battery B is composed of seven pieces of Westerly granite weighing four and a half tons, and is nine

and a half feet high. It is square in form, the base being
fifteen inches deep and three feet eight inches square, and the
finish is a combination of "rustic"—that is, giving the appearance of roughly-hewn natural rock—and hammered work,
the capstone being hammered. The whole is surmounted by a
granite representation of a cannon ball. The die bears the
Second Corps badge and the inscription, "Brown's Battery B,
First R. I. Light Artillery, Second Brigade, Second Corps,
Army of the Potomac."

The memorial of Battery E is located on the easterly side
of the Emmettsburg Road just northerly of Sherfy's Peach
Orchard, that battery having been in the Third Corps and
actively engaged with it on that part of the field in the second
day's fight. As, however, this memorial was dedicated July
3d, 1886, at the time of the Third Corps Reunion, its dedication formed no feature of the Rhode Island Excursion to Gettysburg, hence no further mention of it will be made here.

At the reunions in the summer of 1886, of the several Associations, other than Battery E, having memorials at Gettysburg, committees were appointed to arrange for an excursion
to dedicate the memorials and to visit the various points of
interest on the battlefield. The committees thus appointed
united and formed a single Excursion Committee, its members
being Gen. Horatio Rogers, Gen. Elisha H. Rhodes and Lieut.
Amos M. Bowen of the 2d R. I. Vols., Capt. Benj. H. Child of
Battery A, 1st R. I. L. A., and D. Coit Taylor and Capt. Gideon
Spencer of Battery B, 1st R. I. L. A. Gen. Rogers was appointed chairman, and Mr. Taylor secretary. An excursion
was organized to visit Gettysburg in October, 1886, and all
disposed to join it were invited to do so. Though the Chairman of the Excursion was to preside at all the dedicatory
services, yet otherwise the committee of each Association was
to arrange and carry out the programme at its own memorial.
The details of the excursion will best be shown by the following circulars issued by a Sub Committee or by the Excursion
Manager.

RHODE ISLAND EXCURSION TO GETTYSBURG.

PROVIDENCE, September 16, 1886.

The undersigned, representing the Committee of the Second Rhode Island Volunteers and Batteries A and B, Rhode Island Light Artillery, announce the following in relation to the proposed excursion to the Battle-field of Gettysburg.

The fare from Providence to Gettysburg and return, via New York and Harrisburg, $12.00; the hotel rates at Gettysburg as follows: McClellan House, $1.50 per day; Eagle Hotel, $2.00 per day.

The Excursion will leave Providence, via Stonington Line, Monday, October 11, arriving at Gettysburg, Tuesday, at 6 p.m.; leave Gettysburg, Friday, at 4.45 a. m., arriving in New York at 2 p.m.

Meals going and returning and rides about the Battle-field will be extra.

It is important that the committee be informed immediately if you intend to take the trip, as they are obliged to guarantee the sale of fifty tickets in order to secure the above rates. Please fill out and return the enclosed postal card without delay, writing your name, address and number of tickets you require. Further information will be sent to those agreeing to go. This excursion will include citizens and ladies at the same rate as for the Veterans.

E. H. RHODES, 2d R. I. Vols.,
BENJAMIN H. CHILD, Battery A, R. I. L. A., } Committee.
D. COIT TAYLOR, Battery B, R. I. L. A.,

RHODE ISLAND EXCURSION TO GETTYSBURG.

PROVIDENCE, October 4, 1886.

The following is announced for the information of those intending to join the excursion:

The party will leave Providence, Monday, October 11, at 7.15 p. m., via Stonington Line; leave Gettysburg, Thursday, October 14, at 5.20 p. m., and pass the night in Harrisburg. By presenting your Excursion Ticket at the Ticket Office in Harrisburg you can purchase a Ticket from Harrisburg to Washington and return for $5.00.

The return ticket from Harrisburg to New York will be good until midnight, Thursday, October 21st; the ticket from New York to Providence will be good until October 30th. You can stop over at Philadelphia if you wish.

Tickets will be for sale on and after October 7, at Ticket Office of N. Y., B. & P. R. R. Passenger Station, Exchange Place, Providence, price $12.00; State Room Tickets for Monday night can be purchased from the undersigned at City Hall, Providence, on Saturday and Monday, October 9th and 11th, from 12 to 2 p. m.

Additional Printed Information will be distributed on the train from Providence, Monday Evening.

Procure your tickets early.

E. H. RHODES, Excursion Manager.

RHODE ISLAND EXCURSION TO GETTYSBURG, PENN.,
OCTOBER, 1886.

COMMITTEES.

GEN. HORATIO ROGERS,   GEN. ELISHA H. RHODES,
LIEUT. AMOS M. BOWEN, 2d R. I. Vols.
CAPT. BENJAMIN H. CHILD, Battery A, R. I. L. A.
D. COIT TAYLOR,   CAPT. GIDEON SPENCER,
Battery B, R. I. L. A.

OFFICERS OF THE EXCURSION.

GEN. HORATIO ROGERS, Chairman.   REV. SAMUEL H. WEBB, Chaplain.
D. COIT TAYLOR, Secretary.   GEN. ELISHA H. RHODES, Manager.

ITINERARY.

MONDAY, OCTOBER 11.

7.15 P. M.   Leave Providence, Stonington Line.
9 P. M.   Take Steamer Massachusetts at Stonington.

TUESDAY, Oct. 12.

6.30 A. M.   Arrive at New York.
Breakfast when and where you please. Cross to Jersey City by ferry,

either at Desbrosses' or Courtland street.   A good restaurant will be found at the Jersey City depot.

9.16 A. M.   Train leaves Jersey City, Penn. R. R.

11.30 A. M.   Arrive at Philadelphia.   Twenty minutes for dinner.

11.50 A. M.   Leave Philadelphia.

3.20 P. M.   Arrive at Harrisburg.   Change cars.

3.40 P. M.   Leave Harrisburg.

5.50 P. M   Arrive at Gettysburg.   Select your hotel.

Headquarters at Eagle Hotel.   Rates: Eagle Hotel, $2.00 per day; McClellan House, $1.50 per day.

WEDNESDAY, Oct. 13.

At Gettysburg :   The R. I. Memorials will be dedicated.   Addresses by Gen. Horatio Rogers and others.

Notices giving particulars will be posted at the hotels.

THURSDAY, Oct. 14.

At Gettysburg :   Rides over the Battle-field with guide.   Fare for ride, $1.00.   See notices posted at hotels.

5.20 P. M.   Leave Gettysburg.

7.45 P. M.   Arrive at Harrisburg, and remain over night at the United States Hotel.   Rate, $2.00 per day.

Parties who wish, by presenting their Excursion Tickets at the ticket office, can purchase tickets from Harrisburg to Washington and return for $5.00.

On returning they must leave Harrisburg in time to reach New York before midnight, Thursday, Oct. 21.

FRIDAY, Oct. 15.

7 A. M.   Leave Harrisburg.

10.20 A. M.   Arrive at Philadelphia.

Stop over at Philadelphia if you wish.   Ask conductor for stop-over checks after leaving Harrisburg.

11.15 A. M.   Leave Philadelphia.

2 P. M.   Arrive at New York.

4.30 P. M.   Take Stonington steamboat.   Secure your staterooms early.

SATURDAY, Oct. 16.

2 A. M.   Arrive at Stonington.

3 A. M.   Take cars for Providence.

If you wish you can remain upon the boat and take 7.55 A. M. train for Providence.   The wise and the sleepy will do so.

4.30 or 9.15 A. M.   Arrive in Providence.   " Home, sweet Home."

Tickets good for ten days from Oct. 11.

Information will be given by the Manager at any hour, day or night, " rain or shine."

ELISHA H. RHODES, Excursion Manager.

2

The roster of the excursion as made up by the manager was
as follows :

LADIES.

Mrs. George T. Baker,	Drownville, R. I.
Mrs. Moses B. Chace,	Providence, "
Mrs. Benjamin H. Child,	" "
Mrs. William D. Child,	" "
Mrs. William J. Crossley,	" "
Mrs. Elias M. Jenckes,	" "
Mrs. Edwin R. Jones,	" "
Miss Susie A. Lewis,	" "
Mrs. Alfred O. Makee,	" "
Mrs. George H. Paddock,	" "
Miss Louise F. Peirce,	Auburn, "
Mrs. Robert Robertson,	Central Falls, "
Mrs. T. Mumford Seabury,	Newport, "
Mrs. John P. Sanborn,	" "
Mrs. Richmond J. Stone,	Howard, "
Miss Mabel R. Stone,	" "
Mrs. D. Coit Taylor,	Providence, "
Mrs. Peter Vennerbeck,	" "
Mrs. Josiah T. Warren,	Bristol, "

SECOND RHODE ISLAND VOLUNTEERS.

Arnold, Edwin W.	Corporal	Providence, R. I.
Bowen, Amos M.	First Lieutenant	"
Cook, Lowell C.	Corporal	South Milford, Mass.
Crossley, William J.	Sergeant	Providence, R. I.
Curtis, Joseph B.	Sergeant	"
Horton, Daniel H.	Private	Pawtucket, R. I.
Johnstone, Robert L.	Private	"
Lewis, Charles L. C.	Private	Hope Valley, R. I.
Makee, Alfred O.	Private	Providence, R. I.
Martin, Owen 2d.	Private	"
McDonough, Patrick	Private	Olneyville, R. I.
Nichols, Charles S.	Private	Hope Valley, R. I.
Parkhurst, Albert B.	Private	Woonsocket, R. I.
Prentiss, Edmund F.	Captain	Providence, R. I.
Proctor, Thomas B.	Private	Davisville, R. I.
Rhodes, Elisha H.	Colonel	Providence, R. I.
Robertson, Robert	First Lieutenant	Central Falls, R. I.
Rogers, Horatio	Col. and Bvt. Brig. Gen.	Providence R. I.
Stone, Richmond J.	Sergeant	Howard, R. I.
Warren, Josiah T.	Private	Bristol, R. I.

BATTERY A, FIRST RHODE ISLAND LIGHT ARTILLERY.

Cargill, Charles.........Private....................Providence, R. I.
Child, Benjamin H......First Lieutenant...........   "
Child, William D.......First Sergeant..............   "
Cullin, Timothy........Private ....   "
Greene, Stephen M......Sergeant... ....   "
Jerrolman, James T.....Bugler....................   "
LeWis, James..........Private....................   "
Olney, Amos M.........Quartermaster-Sergeant.....   "

BATTERY B, FIRST RHODE ISLAND LIGHT ARTILLERY.

Delevan, John.........Private....................Brooklyn, N. Y.
Reynolds, Wm. F......Private....................Milford, Mass.
Taylor, D. Coit.........Private....................Providence, R. I.
Whipple, Albert J......Private....................Woonsocket, R. I.

Addeman, Joshua M....Captain, 14th R. I. H. A....Providence, R. I.
Baker, George T........Sergeant, 10th R. I. V......Drownville, R. I.
Chace, Moses B.........Corporal, 10th R. I. V......Providence, R. I.
Chase, Philip S.........Lient., Bat. F, R. I. L. A....   "
Jackson, Richard H... Lieut., 9th N. Y. Vols......   "
Jenckes, Elias M ......Q. M. Sergt. 1st R. I. D. M..   "
Markley, John H.......{ 1st Lieut. and Brevet }..Boston, Mass.
                      { Capt. 2d U. S. Inf'ty, }
Paddock, George H.....Private, 1st. R. I. D. M......Providence, R. I.
Swan, James O.........{ Com. Sergt., 1st R. I. }   "
                      { D. M. and 10th R. I. V. }
Tanner, James A.......Sergt., Bat. E, R. I. L. A....   "

CIVILIANS.

Arnold, Charles   -   -   Providence, R. I.
Briggs, Osmond H. -   .   .   .   -   "
Fisher, Samuel H.   . Hope Valley, R. I.
Johnson, William S.   .   . - Providence, R. I.
Jones, Edwin R.   .   . -   "
Kenyon, William H.   -   - Hope Valley, R. I.
Lowry, William N.   .   .   . - Providence, R. I.
Mathews, Adrian, M. D.,   .   .   . -
Mathews, Franklin, M. D.,   Philadelphia, Pa
Miller, William H. -   .   - Providence, R. I.
Morris, Edward D.   "
Newell, Oscar A. -   - Central Falls, R. I.
Pendleton, Benjamin E.   Hope Valley, R. I.
Pickering, Augustus   -   East Blackstone, Mass.
Sanborn, John P.   -   .   .   .   . - Newport, R. I.
Seabury, T. Mumford -   -   .   "

Straight, Charles T.   -   Pawtucket, R. I.
Toye, Robert G.   Providence, R. I.
Vennerbeck, Peter   -   "
Webb, Rev. Samuel H.   "

The weather upon the excursion was delightfully warm and
clear, except Thursday afternoon, when it was showery, and
the itinerary was faithfully carried out.

On Wednesday, Oct. 13th, at 10 A. M., the party took the
train for Little Round Top station, where it arrived ten minutes later, and a walk of about seven minutes brought it to
the memorial of the 2d R. I. Vols. Amid the rocks and under some trees hard by, the following dedicatory services
were held :

INVOCATION BY REV. SAMUEL H. WEBB,
Chaplain of the Excursion.

Almighty and Everlasting God, forasmuch as without thee we
are not able to please thee, grant us the aid of thy grace in the
services in which we are now to be engaged. We acknowledge thee
as the blessed and only Potentate, the King of kings and Lord
of lords, the Almighty Ruler of nations. We adore and magnify
thy glorious Name for all the great things which thou hast
done for us.   We render thee thanks for the goodly heritage
which thou hast preserved to us. We thank thee for the civil
and religious privileges which we enjoy and for all thy goodness
toward us. May we be duly grateful for thy mercies and for the
services of those whose memory we this day recall. Continue to
us, we beseech thee, the blessings of peace ; restore them to nations deprived of them, and secure them to all the people of the
earth. As we gather this day upon the field of bygone strife,
make us sensible of the great work wrought for the preservation
of our country. May we live in holy obedience to thy righteous
laws, and thus be kept from the guilt of abusing the manifold
blessings bestowed upon us. Defend with thy fatherly care the
orphans and widows. Comfort and relieve all those who are in
trouble, sorrow, need, sickness, or any other adversity. Bless
all in legislative, judicial and executive authority, that they may
have grace, wisdom and understanding so to discharge their duties
as most effectually to promote thy glory, the interests of true

religion and virtue, and the peace, good order and welfare of this land, no longer rent with internal dissension. Lead us by thy Holy Spirit ever to put our trust in thee, ever to honor and obey thee. Imprint upon our hearts a deep and habitual sense of the great truth, that the only security for the continuance of those blessings we enjoy consists in our acknowledgment of thy sovereign and gracious Providence, and in holy and humble submission to the gospel of thy Son Jesus Christ. Restrain, we pray thee, the enemies of peace and union. Give wisdom and strength to all in authority over us, that by their counsel, control and efforts, upheld and guided by thy power and blessing, this Republic may ever be preserved. May truth, duty, union and patriotism ever triumph. May we keep in mind the example of those who so nobly defended our beloved land in her hour of peril, and teach our sons and daughters rightly to esteem the blessings of liberty and freedom. Be with us in our present duties, direct and govern our thoughts, words and deeds in accordance with thy will; and when the warfare of this present life is ended, may we be numbered among those who have their names written in the Lamb's Book of Life. We ask for these things in the name and through the merits and intercession of thy Son, our Lord and Saviour Jesus Christ. Amen.

ADDRESS BY GEN. HORATIO ROGERS,

THE COLONEL COMMANDING THE SECOND RHODE ISLAND VOLUNTEERS AT GETTYSBURG.

Comrades of the late Civil War, Ladies and Gentlemen:

We stand on historic ground. Here rebellion culminated. On this spot the onward march of armed resistance to the Government was stayed. Thus far could it go and no farther. From these hills and plains the waves of civil war rolled backward, and in less than two years disappeared from the face of this fair land forever. The battlefield stretched before our eyes is famous for the results achieved upon it. It is likewise celebrated for its natural beauty; and some of the events that transpired here nearly a quarter of a century ago, for grand scenic and picturesque effects, have rarely been equalled and never surpassed in the annals of the continent.

The bloody struggle in the Devil's Den, the scaling of Little
Round Top and the desperate contest for its possession, the
terrific bombardment of the third of July, the gallant but
fatal charge of Pickett's Division, in which but Pickett himself of all his generals, and a single lieut.-colonel of all his
field officers, escaped unscathed from the annihilation of his
command, are ineffaceably impressed upon the minds of all
beholders, and form one of the most memorable chapters of
our national history. Then, too, the battle fought here was
unique in having been the only one on free soil during the
great conflict between union and secession. All these ele-
ments of interest combine to make this the typical battlefield
of the late war, and Gettysburg has been pictured upon can-
vas and narrated upon paper with a graphic distinctness and
a fullness of detail that has characterized no other scene of
conflict in America. It is apparent, therefore, why this has
been selected as the battlefield of the civil war where all or-
ganizations taking part in the stirring events enacted here
have been invited to erect fitting memorials of their participation. As the colonel of the Second Rhode Island Volunteers at Gettysburg, I have been chosen to take the chief part
in the dedication of its memorial on this historic field, and I
shall strive to make the recital of its services more graphic
by weaving into it my own recollections, which course I trust
will meet with your approval.

After the Chancellorsville campaign, in the spring of 1863,
the Second Rhode Island lay quietly at Falmouth till June
6th, when it proceeded to the banks of the Rappahannock,
for it being apparent to Hooker that Lee was making some
kind of a move, General Sedgwick, of the Sixth Corps, had
been ordered to reconnoitre the south bank of the river, in the
hope of developing the enemy's force, and for this purpose a
pontoon bridge had been thrown across at Franklin's crossing
on the 5th. A thousand men of the brigade, including a detail from the Second Rhode Island, were ordered to report,
without arms, to me at the head of the bridge, at dusk of the
7th, and when it became dark we crossed the river and threw

up a line of entrenchments about a mile long marked out for us by General Warren. We labored all night in silence, having been forbidden to talk or to light a match, and by dawn of day we had constructed a practical cover, which the troops then relieving us found no difficulty in completing under fire.

June 9th, the Second crossed to the Fredericksburg side of the river, where it remained under an occasional shelling till the night of the 13th, when in darkness and in rain descending in torrents it recrossed with the rest of the Sixth Corps, and bade a final farewell to Fredericksburg. It had transpired that Lee was moving northward, so the Army of the Potomac followed, the Sixth Corps being on the extreme left, and forming the rear of the army. June 14 we crossed Potomac creek, halting at Stafford Court House till late in the evening, when we pushed on again, crossing Acquia creek early on the 15th. We marched, and marched, and marched, trudging along by day and by night, now under the heat of a scorching sun, and again under the chill of a driving rain that soaked us to the skin. Night and day, rain and shine, dust and mud were all alike to us, however, as we had to take it as it came, and on we went to Dumfries, then to Occoquan creek, next to Fairfax Station. June 18 we had got as far as Fairfax Court House, and for six days we had a little variety of duty, even if it was not all rest, as the corps was strung along as far as Bristoe Station, guarding the railroad and watching the mountain passes. June 26th we started again, reaching Drainesville that night, crossing the Potomac on pontoons the next day at Edwards Ferry, and camping near Poolesville, in Maryland, the night of the 27th. Onward we pushed the next morning through Poolesville and Barnesville, along the base of Sugar Loaf Mountain, through Whitestone to Percy Mills. The Baltimore and Ohio Railroad was passed on the 29th, and on we went through Newmarket and Ridgeville to Mount Airey. The last day of June we marched through Mount Vernon and Westminster to the neighborhood of Manchester, where, happily, we halted for a day.

The hardships of that march from Fredericksburg, who,

that took it, will ever forget? The fierce rays of the sun that beat upon us the day we reached Dumfries burned into my memory so deeply that they can never be obliterated. O, the utter weariness of going into bivouac at midnight after a long day's march to start again at 3 in the morning! What chafed and tired limbs there were, what aching heads!. Fortunately for me I was a mounted officer, which helped somewhat, but the colonel of the Second Rhode Island was not so much of a martinet but that he could tramp for miles to give foot-sore officers and men a needed lift, and one little drummer boy, but for the rides he got from the mounted officers, would have succumbed entirely. But weariness was not our only misery. Wagon trains were on the move, and baggage was not accessible. For three weeks I did not take off my clothes, and when I did they never went on again, hence it will require no very active fancy to picture our unenviable condition. The fare, too, was in keeping with our other trials. We could not always stop to cook, and, when we were famished enough, raw salt pork spread upon hard tack proved an appetizing combination, which made us, like Oliver Twist, to ask for more. Then, too, as we had no base of supplies, we could ill afford to condemn provisions that would support life, and, unfortunately for us, some of our crackers had been on the peninsula the year before, and had become wormy. Time and again have I broken my hard tack into my coffee, and, scooping off a myriad of worms that rose to the top, contentedly ate the rest, for, fastidious as a man may naturally be, there is nothing like an empty stomach to knock the daintiness out of him. Rough as our experiences were, it was very far from being all wretchedness, however, for the scenery was grand and picturesque, we could sleep at a moment's notice without waking for eight or ten hours if permitted, we could digest the coarsest fare and get hungry enough to enjoy it, the life was adventurous and in the open air, and, above all, we had the consciousness that we were doing our duty.

We spent the last day of June near Manchester, and though more than a score of years has since elapsed, the delight of

that rest to our weary limbs abides like a red-letter day in my
memory. All were wondering what had become of Lee, and
expectation was roused to the highest point. We knew that
rebel cavalry had been hovering round us, as the Second had
had some guarding of wagon trains to do, and I had been
particularly warned of the proximity of Confederate troopers.
Then, too, we had occasionally passed dead cavalrymen that
had fallen in recent skirmishes, so that orders to march were
momentarily looked for. Nine o'clock in the evening came,
but the expected orders had not arrived, and quiet reigned
over the camp. Presently, however, far away and faint in the
distance, though distinctly audible, rang out the assembly
from a single cavalry bugle. I interpreted its meaning instantly, and ordered little Dick Higgins, a drummer boy in
his early teens that was kept at headquarters, to beat the
drummer's call preparatory to the assembly. Some of the
staff listened to me in astonishment, as an aid or an orderly
was always sent from brigade headquarters with orders to
pack up, and taking the responsibility of routing out the regiment and getting it ready to march at that time of night
without orders, struck them as peculiar, to say the least, and
they so intimated. My opinion was that the bugle call was
the sure precursor of the long-expected orders, and as my
staff were officers and gentlemen and I was colonel, no more
comments were made, whatever may have been their thoughts,
so the assembly of the Second Rhode Island Drum Corps
broke sharply forth upon the still night air, much to the sur-
prise of my brother colonels, as no one had as yet received
any orders to move. The men packed up rapidly, and in fifteen or twenty minutes down galloped an orderly with the
anticipated orders, and hardly had he got out of hearing when
the generals began to appear, first the brigade and then the
corps commander, and when General Sedgwick saw the Second
Rhode Island all in line ready to march, he rode up to Colonel
Eustis, commanding the brigade, who was talking to me, and
said : "I am glad to find a regiment in the corps ready to
march. Order it to move out at once!" Thus it was the

3

Second Rhode Island led the corps on that eventful march towards Gettysburg. It was a beautiful, calm night, the atmosphere was soft and balmy, and the moon shed forth a gentle radiance sufficient to light us on our way. We tramped all night with scarcely a halt, and to say that we were tired but faintly expressed our feelings. For one, I was completely and utterly exhausted, and when shortly after sunrise we halted for a little rest and to make coffee, I fell asleep, and slept as heavily as if drugged, so that when General Sedgwick was ready to start I could not be wakened, and another regiment was pushed into my place; and thus the Second Rhode Island lost the head of the corps. When, however, I did at last get my eyes open, it was no small problem to wake up the exhausted and sleep-ridden soldiers. I remember aiding some of the line officers in rousing their men. I had on thick top boots and carried a heavy cavalry sabre, so I would kick a man on one side of me and strike another with my sheathed sabre on the other with force enough to knock a wide-awake person over, and yet my vigorous efforts often needed repetition before the weary souls could be induced to open their eyes.

At last we approached the battlefield, and before reaching it a crowd of stragglers swarmed by us. Indeed, it seemed from the fragmentary mass flocking along as if the whole army must have disintegrated and gone to pieces. There has been much discussion as to the time the Sixth Corps arrived at Gettysburg. General Doubleday and the Comte de Paris, in their accounts of the battle, state that the head of the corps arrived about 2 p. m., while others give a later hour. But whatever the time may have been when we finished our thirty-four-mile march—a march famous in the annals of the war—fighting was going on when we turned off the Baltimore Pike on to Powers's Hill and came to a halt on the battlefield. We rested and made coffee, all the while hearing heavy firing at our left, till after a time our brigade was dispatched in that direction to strengthen our lines near Little Round Top, and we first went into line of battle just back of this memorial.

Here we waited expectantly, listening and watching and wondering, but not being called on to do more. Here we remained till day went out and darkness settled over the combatants, and here we spent the night in line of battle, resting on our arms. How well I recall that night! My headquarters were under a large tree a few paces in rear of the left wing of the regiment, and all night long a throng of wounded in blue and gray were borne along close by us. The groans of the poor fellows were heart-rending, and as I lay at the foot of that tree in the pale moonlight, watching the sad procession, listening to the agonizing sounds and wondering what the final issue of the great struggle we were engaged in was going to be, I could not help thinking of the Duke of Wellington's famous saying, that, next to a defeat, the saddest thing was a victory.

The following morning, July 3d, we were up at break of day, for no one knew what was in store for us. The hours were slipping rapidly away, and we seemed destined to inaction, though very heavy firing was going on far to our right. At last came orders to march. The rebel General Johnston had pierced the Federal lines on Culp's Hill, on the extreme right, the evening before, and had penetrated almost to the Baltimore Pike, spending the night there, so the first effort of the day was to push him back. He held on doggedly, and reinforcements were dispatched to aid the 12th corps, among others our brigade, but he was repulsed before we reached the scene of action, and we had a hot, weary and fruitless march. The scorching heat of that July sun was intense and we suffered greatly. Noon was approaching and quiet pervaded the battlefield. One o'clock came, and the report of two guns broke upon the ear, and directly 134 pieces of Confederate artillery belched forth their pandemonium of sound and destruction. Eighty Federal cannon replied, and it seemed as if Satan and all his cohorts were holding carnival. For nearly two hours this furious cannonade went on, and who ever heard it and witnessed its effects, will never forget it, though like the Wandering Jew he were fated to live forever on the earth.

We were on a plain exposed to the pitiless blast, and before we could get to cover we had quite a distance to traverse. The roar of the guns, the fiendish explosion of shells, the snapping of branches of trees overhead caused by pieces of shell, the fall of stricken men, the hurrying flight of soldiers to cover, the shrinking to earth of those in line of battle that could seek no refuge, the agonized terror of wounded horses dashing along—all made up a scene that must be witnessed to be appreciated. The frantic actions of the injured animals were particularly impressive. Of the many such I recall a particularly fine, strong horse, with his under jaw shot away, tearing along in a frenzy of pain. Next came Pickett's grand charge, and our brigade, ever on the move to threatened points, was hurried along to the place of danger. We passed just in rear of our line of battle, using our eyes and our legs to the utmost of our power. As we were nearing our journey's end a glad shout of triumph broke forth, and ringing cheers travelled along the line toward us. Presently came a crowd of rebel officers and a score or two of captured flags under guard, followed at a short distance by thousands of rebel prisoners being carried to the rear, and then the cause of the shouts and the cheers became apparent, and we, too, took up the joyous sounds, which rolled on down the lines beyond us. Pickett's Division had been annihilated, the Confederate attack had signally failed, and Lee's anticipations of victory had turned into the bitter realization of defeat. The Federal left, right and centre had been successively assailed. At each point it seemed, at times, as if the gray was about to triumph over the blue, but the God of Battles had otherwise decreed, and each time the Confederate assaults had come to naught. We wondered if a counter attack would not be made, and we knew full well that, if made, it would devolve upon the Sixth Corps. The afternoon wore on, however, and the expected move was not ordered, so we watched the sun go down, and again lay down in line of battle to await the coming day, but this time we wondered less as to the outcome of the pending struggle, as we felt that victory was assured.

The morning light of July 4th found us astir, ready for the duties of the day. During the night General Lee drew back his left wing, which encircled our right, thus straightening his line and making it a less aggressive and a better defensive position. Neither side showed any disposition to attack, but the picket lines kept up a constant fire. Early in the day the regiment was ordered down to the Emmetsburg road to support Berdan's sharpshooters on the picket line. To protect the men as much as possible from the constant fusilade going on, I brought the command into line of battle and took it at the double quick the last few hundred yards, and even then one man was wounded. At the Emmetsburg road we hugged mother earth for shelter, our only duty being to support the sharpshooters in our front in case of a Confederate advance, which, however, never came. After a while, the fire became less lively, and we began to look about us. What a sight was spread before our eyes! It was enough to appal the stoutest heart. We lay between the two armies where the fighting had been hot and heavy on the second day, and where the Union fire swept the Confederate lines as they advanced in the famous charge the day before. We commanded an extensive view, and dead horses and stricken men lay in myriads about us. Blue uniforms and gray were commingled there, the wearers having joined other ranks where those colors ceased to have significance. We seemed to have entered the very Court of Death. The dead were everywhere. The ground, in places, was fairly carpeted with them. Just back and to the left of us, in an orchard, was a Union battery, complete as to officers, artillerists and horses, save that all were stiff and stark in death. It was in position for action. The limbers were in rear of the pieces with the horses hitched to them. The men grasped their rammers and their lanyards. Everything about it seemed entire, save that all that had been instinct with life two short days before, had been stricken down. Dotting the field one could see little white flags where wounded men had raised a handkerchief on a ramrod as a signal of distress and as an indication that they were not dead, so that assistance might go to them. Stretcher-men, of course, were busy, and we lay quietly and watched the sad and sickening sight. Indeed, prostrate forms were so numerous that, as we could not be relieved till after nightfall to avoid exposure, I had to dismount and lead my horse when we left the field for fear of stepping on human bodies. The sun shone fiercely anon, and then the rain would descend in torrents, and this continued at intervals throughout the day. The atmospheric effect upon the dead, therefore, was extremely rapid, and the stench was terrible.

War affords many striking incidents, and one occurred on that grim tour of picket duty that illustrated alike the value and the virtue of Masonic brotherhood, and shed a soft and hallowing influence over the ghastly surroundings of that scene of strife. Many dead lay in the Emmetsburg road in front of us, and just opposite the right of the regiment, stretched out at full length, was the lifeless form of a Confederate colonel. His was a fine, manly figure, and he was smitten down in the prime of life. It was ascertained from a Masonic certificate in his pocket, which I hold in my hand, that his name was Joseph Wasden, and that he was a member of Franklin Lodge, No. 11, of Warrenton, Ga. Thereupon it was determined that this deceased brother, an enemy in life, that had been stricken down far from his home and loved ones, should be buried by fraternal hands, and the blue uniforms gathered round the gray as a squad of the Second Rhode Island, under the direction of Captain Thomas Foy, a Past Master of King Solomon Lodge, No. 11, of East Greenwich, raised the inanimate form in their arms and bore it carefully two or three hundred yards to the right, where they tenderly and reverently buried it on the south side of Codori's barn, the opposing picket shots serving as minute guns. Several years ago, at one of our regimental reunions, I requested Capt. Foy to send me the certificate, and to give me the details of this burial in which he was the chief participant ; and I extract some sentences from the letter he soon afterwards sent me. He wrote : "I saw Corporal Archie Stalker the day after the reunion, but he was unable to remember the names of the privates who assisted us at the burial of Colonel Wasden.

"It should be mentioned that Corporal Stalker (who is an excellent amateur letterer), by my direction, prepared a headstone (sic) out of the top of an ammunition box, and carved the Colonel's name, rank and regiment upon it, and erected it at the head of the grave, and the corporal informed me that he had conversed with the author of a picture of the battlefield of Gettysburg (Carpenter, I think,) who asserted that he saw such a headstone when he was on the field taking notes.

"You doubtless remember that the grave was made contiguous to a barn. Well, in that barn at the time there were a lot of wounded rebels, a part of whom claimed to be members of Wasden's regiment. I requested them, if they lived to get home, to inform the friends of Colonel Wasden that he was decently buried, and by a Mason."

The grave was so well marked that many people here in Gettysburg remember it, and a year ago, or more, when I was here last, an officer of Good Samaritan Lodge, No. 336, located here, informed me that members of that Lodge assisted in removing the remains when subsequently exhumed and forwarded to his friends. Being myself a Mason and interested to know something more of the subject of this romantic incident, a few weeks since I addressed a note to the Master of Franklin Lodge, No. 11, of Warrenton, Ga., and this is his reply :

"ORDINARY'S OFFICE, WARREN COUNTY,
"WARRENTON, GA., Sept. 22, 1886.

"To HORATIO ROGERS, Esq., Providence, R. I. :

"*My Dear Sir and Bro.*—Your letter of inquiry reached me yesterday. I must confess that I was touched by its perusal. I have been a Mason about forty-two years. I have been Master of our Lodge, Franklin Lodge, No. 11, a great many times. Under the circumstances it affords me unusual pleasure to comply with your request, at least in part. Joseph Wasden enlisted as a volunteer in this county, 31st day of August, 1861. He was captain of the company. He was afterwards promoted Major, then Lieutenant-Colonel, and then Colonel of the 22d Georgia Regiment. He was killed on the second day of the fight, and on the 2d day of July, 1863.

" Some tidings of the kindness and tender offices shown his body had reached here, but nothing so satisfactory as that which your letter contains. I am glad to know that his body fell into such hands, and that the blessed principles of our ancient craft are not to be forgotten or eclipsed by the clangor of arms, the din of war, or anything else, and that the nerveless embrace of death is no barrier to a Mason's charity. Colonel Wasden was about 35 years of age. He was a poor boy, did not receive much education, but had spirit and ambition, and was destined to distinction if he had lived. He was a lawyer by profession, and was rising slowly, but surely, in the practice.

" His wife—he had no children—was a northern lady, and I suppose at this time is at St. Paul's, Minnesota. If his body was sent anywhere, it must have been sent to her in some northern State. It was not brought to Georgia. Mrs. Wasden's *given name* was Marion. The Colonel's sword is in this county now, in possession of a friend of Mrs. Wasden, with whom she lived after the death of her husband until the war was over. I do not know that Mrs. W. is living.

" I have to-day seen Captain Beall of Colonel Wasden's regiment. He says the Colonel was rising fast in the army. His superior officers had their eyes fixed on him, and he would soon have been promoted still higher.

" In conclusion, I am glad to assure you and all connected with that transaction, that your kindness was not unworthily bestowed.

" I am very truly and fraternally yours, etc.,

" R. W. HUBERT,
" W. M. Franklin Lodge, No. 11."

The Twenty-Second Georgia was in Wright's Brigade, Anderson's Division of A. P. Hill's Corps, and it lost at Gettysburg 21 killed and 75 wounded, and Colonel Wasden must

have been killed late in the afternoon of the second day's
fight.*

When on picket we all felt sure that Lee was retreating, for
all day long we could hear the rumble of his wagon trains.
After dark we rejoined our brigade, but the next morning,
July 5th, the Second Rhode Island was ordered to report to
General Neil, and be temporarily attached to his brigade,
which led the pursuit of the Confederate army, for the latter
had departed during the night. The rebel wounded were
everywhere. . We overtook them on the road; the barns and

* Through the courtesy of Dr. J. W. C. O'Neal, of Gettysburg, the following, in regard
to the removal of Col. Wasden's remains from Gettysburg to Georgia, has been obtained :

"844 N. 10th St., Phila., Oct. 27th, 1886.

"DEAR DOCTOR: It affords me pleasure to gratify your desire for information concerning the exhumation and reburial of the remains of Col. J. Wasden, 22d Ga. Reg't, who was
killed at Gettysburg, July —, 1863.

"During the summer of 1871, per contract with the Savannah Memorial Asso'n, I exhumed
the remains of Col. Wasden, and those of one hundred Georgians, who had been buried on
the battlefield at Gettysburg; and shipped the same to the S. M. Asso'n, by whom they
were re-interred in the cemetery at Savannah, Ga.

"The grave, on the head-board of which was conspicuously marked 'Col. J. Wasden,
22nd Ga. Reg.,' was located on east side of Emmettsburg road, just inside the fence, and
near the south end of Codori's barn. The grave was single and alone. I exhumed the remains of Col. W. and packed them in a large box, No. 5, in company with those of eight
other Georgians whose names were known, as their graves had been marked.

"The remains were not packed separately in small boxes, but collectively in large boxes,
by direction from the S. M. A. to meet the limited capacity of the Soldiers' Lot in the cemetery. Any further information which may be desired concerning these remains can be received by addressing Mrs. John Williamson, President of the S. M. Asso'n, Savannah, Ga.

"I am fraternally yours,

"R. B. WEAVER.

"To Dr. J. W. C. O'Neal, Gettysburg, Pa."

"DEAR DOCTOR: I trust that the enclosed note may meet your want. If I understood
you correctly, you desired a note showing that I removed the remains of Col. W., by whose
authority, and where they could be found—or, rather, where they were re-buried. These
three facts my letter contains.

"You will understand why Col. W.'s remains were not packed in a separate box. I sent
a list of the names to the Association, so that by referring to the list they can ascertain in
which one of the 8 boxes any one of the remains, sought after, may be found, for the names
on the list correspond with the number on each box. Col. W.'s bones are in box No. 5, with
the bones of 8 other comrades, and among which are the bones of Lt.-Col. D. R. E. Winn,
4th Ga. (You mind he was buried at Blocker's, and it was his gold-plate teeth that I paid
$5 for through you. You expressed the teeth and receipt to me, and I expressed them
to Savannah.) I will be pleased to reply to any inquiry you may make at any time. Hoping
that you may continue in good health,

"I am, with best wishes,   R. B. W."

Dr. Weaver is at present Demonstrator of Anatomy in the Hahnemann Medical School,
Philadelphia.

4

houses we passed were filled with them ; and it seemed as if there was no end to them. More or less able-bodied stragglers were picked up, and I recall the tone and manner of one of them as I was giving orders how to guard a squad of a dozen or fifteen that I had in charge. I spoke of them as " Gray-backs," and he smilingly looked up and said : " Colonel, I never heard us called by that name before." We followed Lee down to Virginia, capturing some prisoners, skirmishing heavily at Funkstown, where several of the regiment were wounded, and where we thought we were going to fight. The Confederate army was allowed to cross to Virginia practically unmolested, and the Gettysburg campaign ended.

The casualties in the Second Rhode Island in the famous battle fought here, were utterly disproportioned to the services rendered and the sufferings endured, as it had but one man killed and five wounded. The smallness of the loss, however, was largely due to the regiment's having been studiously spread out while it was exposed to the furious cannonade of July 3d, so that a bursting shell could hit but a single man, whereas one of the other regiments of the brigade that marched with closed ranks lost nearly five times as many as we. Another favoring circumstance was that our brigade, like most of the Sixth Corps, was in the reserve, and this at once con-duced to our safety and afforded us superior opportunities to observe what was transpiring around us ; but it was, neverthe-less, a trying and onerous position, as reserves are called on in emergencies, and are, therefore, of the flower of the army, that can be relied on at a pinch. Napoleon's Old Guard was always in his reserve. It is an infinitely harder strain upon the nerves of men to watch and wait, often enduring a fire they are forbidden to return, than it is to actually fight, for the pent-up feelings find relief in the excitement of action.

This, Comrades, and Ladies and Gentlemen, constitutes the record of the Second Rhode Island at the great battle fought here, and it is to perpetuate this record that the Gettysburg Battlefield Memorial Association has invited us to place a memorial upon this field. In response to that invitation this

bronze surmounted granite, bearing, besides its other orna-
mentation, the arms of the State and an appropriate inscription, has been erected at the joint expense of the State of
Rhode Island and the Second Rhode Island Veteran Association, and we confide it to your keeping. Mr. Secretary, as the
representative of the Gettysburg Battlefield Memorial Association, to guard with the other memorials of both opponents
on this historic field, that have been, and are to be, placed
here, and which for all time to come will attest the constancy
and the valor with which this people, North and South, con-
tended for their principles. But, while this memorial is intended to commemorate the honorable part we of the Second
Rhode Island bore in the most memorable struggle of the late
civil war, it is intended to represent nothing more. The din of
battle is over, the animosities of war have ceased, and Yank
and Reb., Unionist and Secesh, Federal and Confederate, have
laid aside both their arms and their bitterness, and having
fought their differences out like men, now greet each other as
fellow-countrymen, and point with pride to a common flag as
the ægis of our liberties.

ADDRESS BY HON. JOHN M. KRAUTH,

SECRETARY OF THE GETTYSBURG BATTLEFIELD MEMORIAL ASSOCIATION.

Veterans of Rhode Island, Ladies and Gentlemen :—It affords me very great pleasure, as the representative of the
Gettysburg Battlefield Memorial Association, to receive into
our care and custody this monument. This beautiful struc-
ture, as already stated, has been erected by a grateful State,
supplemented by the subscriptions of the survivors of the
regiment, to commemorate and perpetuate the gallant deeds
of the gallant men who here fought for the integrity of the
Union. I can assure you that it will give this Association and
its successors the greatest pleasure to see that no harm shall
come to these monuments, to so guard them that they shall
be preserved in their beauty to be handed down to the latest
generations, in order that they who come to this great field

of battle may see what the citizens of your State and the citizens of the northern portion of the country sacrificed for this country. Again we thank you and congratulate you on your distinguished service, and renew our assurances that we shall guard this memorial to perpetuate the services and gallantry of the Second Rhode Island Volunteers.

BENEDICTION BY CHAPLAIN WEBB.

The Peace of God, which passeth all understanding, keep your hearts and minds in the knowledge and love of God, and of his Son Jesus Christ, our Lord; and the blessing of God Almighty, the Father, the Son, and the Holy Ghost, be amongst you and remain with you always. Amen.

The party then proceeded by train to Hancock Station, whence a few minutes' walk brought it to the memorials of Batteries A and B, where the following dedicatory services were had, beginning at the memorial of Battery A.

INVOCATION BY CHAPLAIN WEBB.

Most Mighty and Merciful Father, we come before thee in an humble sense of our own unworthiness, beseeching thee to assist us in the solemn duties of the present hour. Be with us as thou hast promised to be with those who make their petitions in thy Son's name. Give us wisdom from on High that we may faithfully observe thy laws and do thy will. May we preserve evermore the remembrance of our departed comrades. May their heroic deeds be held in grateful esteem by those who enjoy the blessings they helped to gain for our country. Let thy good Spirit abide in our midst that so we may perform faithfully and well the duties of this day. As we gather here in thy presence, help us to realize the greatness of the work performed by those whose bravery we commemorate. May the good example of our fallen comrades be had in mind. May we wisely improve our opportunities and shew forth thy glory by upholding the principles of equity, freedom and patriotism. Have mercy upon our land and all who dwell therein. Keep them from all evil, prosper their efforts to promote peace and happiness on earth. Look in mercy

upon the distressed of this and other lands. Bless all in authority over us, and so rule their hearts and strengthen their hands
that they may punish wickedness and vice, and maintain thy true
religion and virtue. May we in our present life serve well the
great Captain of man's salvation, and in thine own good time be
received into the Church triumphant. All which we ask through
Jesus Christ, our Lord and Saviour. Amen.

ADDRESS BY LIEUT. BENJAMIN H. CHILD,

Who Served as a Sergeant with Battery A, at the Battle of Gettysburg, in which he was Wounded.

Mr. Chairman, Comrades, and Ladies and Gentlemen:

Hardly had the first call for three months' men, in 1861,
been responded to, when the military authorities of Rhode
Island contemplated the organization of the Second Regiment
of Infantry and a second battery. Enrollments progressed
rapidly, and but a few days after not less than 400 men were
desirous of linking their fortunes with the battery. The arm-
ory on Benefit street in Providence, was the rendezvous of
men from sunrise till late at night eager to acquire the knowledge of military tactics, foot drill and manual of the piece.
Some men were so anxious as to come before daylight, and
would not leave in the evening until the armorer persuaded
them to. We expected to get mustered into three months'
service, but the Federal Government by issuing a call for
75,000 men for not less than three years, left no other alter-
native but to serve the said term. At last the day that was
to transform us from citizens to soldiers arrived, the required
number to man the battery being selected, out of 400, by Sur-
geon Wheaton. On the 5th day of June, 1861, at 5 o'clock
p. m., we were mustered into the service of the United States
for three years, unless sooner discharged. The 19th inst.
witnessed our departure for Washington, D. C. On July 9th
a sad accident occurred at section drill. Through some unknown cause a limber-chest of Lieut. Vaughn's section, filled
with cartridges, exploded, while Gunner Morse and Privates

Brown and Freeman were mounted. Morse and Brown died within an hour. Freeman was badly injured, but recovered after a lingering sickness. Sunday, July 21st, we received our first baptism by fire at the battle of Manassas Plains, or Bull Run. We advanced steadily from Centreville until arriving at Bull Run and Sudley Church, where a halt was made to rest our men and horses. At this moment the brave Rhode Island Infantry, commanded by Col. Slocum, came upon the enemy, who were concealed in the woods. Their situation was getting critical; the report of cannon and musketry followed in rapid succession. Our battery, after passing Sudley Church, commenced to trot in great haste to the place of combat. At this moment Gen. McDowell rode up in a state of great excitement, shouting to Capt. Reynolds : " Forward with your light battery." This was entirely needless, as we were going at high speed, for all were anxious to come to the rescue of our Second Regiment. In quick time our guns were unlimbered, with or without orders. No matter, it was done, and never did better music sound to the old Second Regiment than the quick report of our guns, driving back the enemy. For nearly forty minutes our battery and the Second Regiment defended that ground before any other troops were brought into action. The setting sun of that day found the fragments of our army not only in full retreat, but in a complete rout, leaving most of the artillery in the hands of the enemy, our battery being the only six-gun battery taking all its guns off of the battlefield, two guns being in a disabled condition. Five of our guns were lost at the Cub Run bridge. The following morning we arrived in Washington with one gun and a six-horse team, all that was left of our battery. We lost one man killed and several wounded and prisoners. On the 13th of August, the State having organized a regiment of light artillery, we were no longer called the Second Battery, but Battery A, First Rhode Island Light Artillery. The battery was engaged in most of the battles in the Peninsula campaign of 1862.

September 2, 1862, we were in the Second Corps at the

second Bull Run. We left Fairfax Court House at 8 a. m., forming in line of battle on Flint Hill. Not being attached, our line
of march was resumed. Soon a rebel battery opened on our rear
directly from the town. Gen. Sumner, commanding the Second Corps, ordered one section of our battery and the First
Minnesota Infantry, commanded by Col. Sulley, to take position, planting the two guns of the right section on each side
of the road. About dusk the enemy appeared. We could
hear the unlimbering of the artillery. At that moment we
opened lively with shell and canister, while Col. Sulley threw
his regiment across the road and kept up a brisk musketry
fire on the advancing cavalry of the enemy. Being unable to
use their artillery, the rebels retreated. The First Minnesota
lost seven men killed. One of our limber chests was upset
and the pole broken, injuring one man and a horse. Col.
Sulley was anxious to fall back, and advised our captain to
lose no time, and, if necessary, to abandon the gun. Capt.
Tompkins replied he would carry the gun along or share its
fate. We all went to work tying the two guns and limbers
together, and they were carried safely away.

September 17th — Battle of Antietam or Sharpsburg.
Since 4 a. m. the battle has raged furiously. Gen. Hooker
gained some ground early in the morning, but was wounded
soon after the ball opened. Our battery was ordered to take
position close to Hooker's line. The battlefield wore a terrific
aspect at our arrival. Before reaching our designated position
we had to pass through the enemy's artillery fire for nearly a
mile. Two of our men were wounded before getting into
position. While marching through a corn-field we saw one
of our batteries entirely demolished, and hundreds of dead and
wounded, both the blue and the gray, lay everywhere around
us. Crossing the field we were heartily cheered by the famous
old Sedgwick's division, which was advancing on the enemy
like veterans. We took our position near a cemetery and in
front of a burning farm house—a place already fought for all
the morning, as could be seen by the dead and wounded strewn
around. We relieved a battery of Gen. Hooker's command,

and were supported by two companies of the Twenty-eighth Pennsylvania Infantry commanded by a sergeant. Here we fought steadily against infantry and artillery for four hours and a half. At one time our situation was very critical. The enemy, after driving Gorman's brigade on our right, came charging from that direction. We used double canister. There was a time when half of the battery was compelled to cease firing. The order " Limber to the rear " was given, but, fortunately, not heard, as it would have resulted in the certain capture of the battery. At this critical turn Capt. Tompkins called on our infantry support to advance, which they did, enabling us to load again. The enemy failing to take the battery, retreated slowly, leaving a battle flag behind, which by right should have been given to the battery, as it fell before the infantry advanced. Our ammunition giving out, Capt. Tompkins sent word to be relieved. Our bugler, John Leach, deserves due mention here for carrying notice through the hottest fire, regardless of his personal safety, to bring rescue to his comrades. Shortly afterwards, Battery G, Rhode Island, came to relieve us. We left our position under a heavy fire of the enemy's batteries, leaving our dead and wounded behind. Battery G was driven from the position we had held for four hours, when the ground was taken by the enemy. Our losses were : killed—Sergt. Reed, Privates Lawrence, Bosworth and Stone, and 13 wounded, and 9 horses killed. The follwing morning Lieut. Jeffrey Hazard with eight men tried to obtain the bodies of our killed, but was not successful, as the enemy's sharpshooters fired at our approach. Later in the day the bodies were recovered in a mutilated state, and buried in the evening in the presence of the battery.

December 13th — Battle of Fredericksburg, Va. Firing commenced about 11 a. m. Capt. Tompkins, having been promoted to major, left the battery, and after making a farewell speech to the boys, introduced our new commander, Capt. Wm. A. Arnold. Shortly after, the command " Forward !" was given, and we took our position on the outskirts of the town. Shot and shell were ploughing through the street already. We took position on the road leading to St. Mary's Heights, and we kept up a constant fire during the afternoon. Owing to our position being protected by houses, our losses were small. Private Hicks was shot through both feet, rendering amputation of both members necessary. On June 14th, 1863, the Second Corps left its position in front of Fredericksburg, Va., for Gettysburg.

Let there be a lasting place in our memory for those who sleep forever on the blood-stained fields of Virginia, Maryland and Pennsylvania—not forgetting comrades Lonnegan, Zimnila, Creamer and Higgins, who were killed on this very ground and now rest in yonder cemetery.*

.Comrades, until within the past few days. I had expected our old commander, Capt. William A. Arnold, to be present with us on this occasion. Instead of coming, however, he has sent a communication giving an account of the battery's doings on the eventful days of July 2d and 3d, 1863, wishing it to be read at the dedication of the battery's memorial, and I will accordingly read it.

CAPT. ARNOLD'S REMINISCENCES.

To the Surviving Members of Battery A, First R. I. Light Artillery, that meet on the historical field of Gettysburg to dedicate a monument erected on the ground occupied by the Battery on the 2d and 3d of July, 1863.

I assumed command of Battery A on the 13th of December, 1862, in the streets of Fredericksburg, Va., the battery being in the Second Corps, Army of the Potomac, and always remained in that grand old corps. The company and myself were com-

---

* The bodies of the following named Rhode Island dead are buried in the National Cemetery at Gettysburg, viz:

1 Charles Powers,	Co. C, 2d R. I. Vols.	8 John Greene,	Bat. B, 1st R.I.L.A.
2 Patrick Lonnegan,	Bat. A, 1st R.I.L.A.	9 David R. King,	" "
3 John Higgins,	" "	10 Ira Bennett,	" "
4 John Zimnila,	" "	11 William Beard,	Bat. E, "
5 Corp. Henry H. Ballou, Bat. B,	"	12 Francis H. Martin,	" "
6 Alfred G. Gardner,	" "	13 Alvin Hilton,	" "
7 Corp. William Jones,	" "	14 Ernest Simpson,	" "

5

parative strangers to each other. Confidence was established
between us in that battle, and as far as I know, that confidence
was never impaired. As is well known to you, Gen. Hooker succeeded Gen. Burnside in command of the Army of the Potomac.
Shortly after Gen. Hooker took command he issued an order
for the inspection of the entire army. Batteries that passed
an A1 inspection would be allowed one officer and five privates leave of absence at the same time. Battery A came
within the list, and it always maintained that high reputation.

The army left the front of Fredericksburg, Va., to find the
enemy. They were found at Gettysburg. The battle of the
first day of July took place while we were at Taneytown, Md.
As is well known, Gen. Hancock was sent forward to Gettysburg. Gen. Gibbon took temporary command of the corps.
We moved that night to within a few miles of the field. The
battery was assigned to the division of Gen. Alex. Hays, and
arrived upon the field with that division at daylight on the
morning of the 2d. It was supported by the First Delaware
and Fourteenth Indiana infantry regiments. Battery I, First U.
S. Artillery, commanded by Lieut. Woodruff, was on the right,
and Battery A, Fourth U. S. Artillery, commanded by Lieut.
Cushing, was on the left. Both of those gallant young officers
were killed. The battery was on the ridge to the left of the
cemetery, and immediately in front of Gen. Meade's headquarters, which were on the Taneytown road. It kept that
position during the two days and until the battle was over,
and then withdrew badly shattered, to make room for a fresh
battery, the ammunition being entirely exhausted. The
morning of the 2d was rather quiet; some artillery firing.
About midway between the position of the battery and the
enemy was the Emmetsburg road, on both sides of which
were fences. The rebel skirmishers, under cover of the fences,
picked off some of the men of the centre section, about dis-
abling the right gun of that section. I asked to have our
skirmish line withdrawn. When done, several rounds of
canister were fired at the fences. No further trouble was
experienced from that quarter. There was more or less ar-

tillery work during the day, we blowing up a caisson of the
enemy in our front. The advance of the Third Corps caused
the most desperate fighting. Battery A, from its position,
took its part. The morning of the third was quiet and ominu-
ous. In the forenoon it was noticed that artillery shots came
from new places in the enemy's line, shots being fired to
get the range. The fact was, they expected to destroy our
batteries, preparatory to a charge of their infantry. This
was not accomplished. Suddenly, about 11.30 or 12 o'clock,
they opened from all their guns on the Second and Third Corps,
to which we all replied. This lasted about one hour, and
nothing was ever heard like it before, or in after battles. The
men of Battery A sprang to their guns and did their part in
a noble manner. During this time we lost most of our men
and horses. It was a terrible ordeal, but bravely borne. The
firing of the enemy suddenly ceased when we ceased firing,
and, as the smoke rose from the field, it was seen that the
enemy were advancing their infantry on a charge. Three
lines of infantry emerged from the woods. As they arrived
out on the open field it was a beautiful sight, and one ever to
be remembered. They came as if on parade, with the green
grass, their red battle flags flying, the sun shining on their
bayonets, the officers riding up and down behind the lines to
keep them closed up—a sight never to be forgotten. There was
not a sound until the first line reached the Emmetsburg road,
when the guns on Round Top and from the Third Corps played
upon their right flank, and we all gave them a fire in front.
This flank fire caused them to crowd to the left, and the whole
force of the charge came upon the second corps. Their lines
did not look as pretty from the Emmetsburg road up. The
enemy met with a crushing defeat. Battery A was completely disabled by the loss of men and horses, and much
material destroyed, and taken from the field.

The faces of all men on that field were very noticeable with
an expression of determination on them to do or die right there.
They did do, and many died right there. The enemy met with
a repulse from which they never recovered.

After all was over, the next day or two, I was directed to
take the material from Battery A, Fourth United States Artillery, the men and horses from Battery B, First Rhode Island, to put the battery into moving condition. This was done,
and the battery performed its part afterwards. It was a fa-
vorite with such generals as Couch, Howard, Alex. Hayes,
Birney, Barlow, Gibbon, and Hancock, the magnificent commander of the grand old Second Corps, to which we had the
honor to belong. We all remember Fredericksburg, Gettysburg, the Wilderness, Spottsylvania, Cold Harbor. It is almost impossible to tell the number of engagements and battles
the battery was engaged in.

It was enlisted for three years, not during the war. The
term of enlistment expired at Cold Harbor, Va., on the 6th
of June, 1864. It was kept up to the extreme front until
almost the last hour of its enlistment. The battery—what
was left of it—was turned over to Lieutenant Dwight, and I
started for Providence with fifty-three men, all that remained
of 150 originally enlisted. During the time that I commanded
the battery, from December, 1862, to the muster out in 1864,
not one man died from disease. The men lost were killed in
battle, a record to be proud of. I often wonder how many of
the fifty-three men that came home with me, are alive to-day,
and how many have passed over the river to join their comrades that went before. We are all growing older, and in a
few years none will be left to tell the tale, but this monument
will last as long as granite will stand to perpetuate the memory of those who fought and died there to save their country
in its extreme peril ; and when we are gone it will be a blessed
history to hand down to our children.

The State of Rhode Island is a small one in territorial
limits, but it did not have a small place in the war, and by
the erection of these monuments on the field of Gettysburg
she takes a position with the larger States, and the care which
she took of her soldiers makes one proud to be a native of the
State.

I regret exceedingly that I shall not be able to be with you on the memorable occasion, but I leave it in the hands of the old comrades who were always brave and true, and it will be well done.

The following address was prepared for the occasion by Mr. William D. Child, who served as a private in Battery A at the battle of Gettysburg, though lack of time prevented its delivery.

Mr. Chairman, Comrades and Friends of Battery A : The field of Gettysburg is still a ground which cannot be trod without emotion.

Although a generation of men has come upon the stage since the events which have placed the name of this beautiful Pennsylvania borough in history as the scene of one of the most terrific and sanguinary battles of the world, to be mentioned as long as the names of Thermopylæ, of Balaklava, or of Waterloo, are spoken, and perhaps beyond, for history will not forget that the emancipation and freedom of a race was a grand and controlling factor in that problem, yet to you, comrades, who come to this field now for the first time, to you, the cycle of whose years has doubled and commenced its second course since those mighty events which gave to you and yours forever a share in its glory, tell me, does there not crowd upon the memory a train of thoughts so tender, so proud, and yet so vivid, that they seem like the events of a year but just agone?

To the soldier who escaped its perils, and to the student of history who understands in the light of events the conditions, which obtained on both sides the bayonet guarded line, of the reasonable rising hopes of that monstrous fallacy of secession, and of the still hopeful but well-nigh discouraged loyalty of the North, the mention of this field recalls not only a vivid picture of heroism and of terror, but of a period in the history of that tremendous four years' struggle, when the opposing theories represented by the two contending hosts, who met almost by accident here—theories which had long since passed

beyond the domain of statesmanship—had been relegated to
the last dread arbitrament of the sword, and upon this spot
between two gigantic armies almost equal in numbers, both
ably marshalled, were to find, the one, either an opening
grave or the first tangible sign of a resurrection morn.

A just conception of the battle of Gettysburg, with all its
momentous consequences for weal or woe to the cause we
loved, cannot be had without considering the salient points,
at least, of the immediate causes which led thereto. It may
be doubted if this republic of ours, since its birth 'mid the
throes of war, e'er saw a darker hour than that which pre-
ceded the dawn of the first of July, '63. You are all familiar
with that history, and I shall speak but briefly thereon, from
the private soldier's standpoint.

Two years and more had elapsed since the first three years'
contingent had taken the field and commenced the mighty
preparation of drill and discipline which was destined in the
later and closing years of the struggle to permeate the mass
like an inspiration, while of the original, whose names were
borne upon the rolls, but a small fraction remained. The
heroes and the victims of the early "Bull Run" had all but
lost their identity as such, and the Army of the Potomac had
been born.

A soldier from the West had been summoned to its command, and no lover ever transferred his allegiance of mind
and soul to the object of his first passion more wholly and
with more honest purpose than did that army tender to him
its devotion and its blood. To it and to him was entrusted
at first the protection of our own capital, and later the sub-
jection of the capital of the Confederacy.—a complex and
gigantic duty,—and history will tell how it was performed.

On Washington's birthday, 1862, the army strikes its tents,
and then commences a series of five chapters in its history,
namely: the peninsular campaign, the Pope defeat, the
semi-victory of Antietam, the failure of Fredericksburg, and
the blunder at Chancellorsville, all written in letters of blood,
and, with one possible exception, all covered with the pall of

defeat. Meanwhile at home the voluntary enlistments had stopped, and the wheel of the draft-box had commenced. Copperheadism, now becoming rampant, had just shown its teeth at Springfield, Ill. (June, '63,) in a convention representing half a million of men, whose sworn and bounden duty it was to deter enlistments, to encourage desertions, and in every possible manner to chock the wheels of Federal success, whether in the field, the senate chamber, or the streets of our cities and hamlets, every one of which, almost, had sent its representative to the front.

Wherever men congregated its hideous counsels were heard, and broken-hearted mothers and gray-haired fathers went back to their homes with the despair born of the momentary thought that perhaps their sacrifices had been in vain.

Our letters from home did not betray this, thanks and honor to the hands and hearts that could write through their burning tears those epistles so full of faith, and hope, and love. Who shall say what was their effect upon this sanguine field? and, to them, does there not belong a part of its glory?

Aside, then, from these letters from home, sometimes interrupted for weeks, but always acting like a tonic when received, there was not much encouragement to be found in a review of the past. We had seen regiments and companies about us decimated by one-half and more of their numbers; we looked in vain for many familiar faces, whether he were a commander or a messmate; and for thousands of these absentees, the graves which marked our paths from the Potomac to the Pennsylvania line, alone could answer.

Within a period of ten months the fourth commander of the army in regular succession had given way to the fifth, and now in the presence of a buoyant and exultant enemy, whom, to use a very mild term, we had grown to respect.

One of Gen. Meade's initial orders concludes with this sentence: "Corps and other commanders are authorized to order the instant death of any man who fails in his duty this hour."

Upon what hypothesis can the language of this sentence be based other than that he and his advisers with the government at Washington felt and knew that, in the impending struggle, it was then or never for the army of the Potomac, and all that hinged thereon? Did that army ever before receive such an order? Did it ever afterwards? Not that the speaker remembers or can find. Is the deduction, then, in the premises, not perfectly fair which concludes that, with the highest authorities, the conviction had obtained, that as that army answered for itself on this field, so would history answer for the preservation or dismemberment of the Union. Gen. Lee and his advisers, in contemplating the practicability of this invasion, had taken all these considerations and many more into the account. There were evidences to them that the time had arrived for the Confederacy to strike but one more determined and successful blow upon the all but fainting head and theory of popular government. Let them but plant their banners at Philadelphia, with its stores and treasure, and Washington be cut off by bayonet line from its people at the North, when out from Baltimore would come to their relief thousands of armed men who were waiting sullenly, but hopefully, for the hour.

New York city, which at the behest of secession had already had the proposition of withdrawal from the Union and establishing herself as a free city, made through the person of its mayor (Fernando Wood), was now wrangling over the constitutionality of the draft, and, if we may believe our own conclusions, was ready at that moment for anything which promised its withdrawal. Foreign complications were trying the mettle and genius of our state-craft. England, the powerful, and France, the boastful, waited with undisguised impatience for the hour of our doom to strike, while the enemies of the republic everywhere rejoiced in the belief that its dissolution was at hand. With the commencement of the year the edict of emancipation had gone forth from the hand and heart of that noblest soul of all the productions of those troublous times. To it and its ultimatum our army stood committed. It was for them now to write with their swords, their bayonets, and their lanyards, what the great Lincoln had written with the pen. Its immortality hinged not more on its conception than on its support; its realization now depended on the fate of battles. In the months and years of war through which we had just passed, there had obtained to some extent throughout the army an aversion to any measure of this kind. This aversion had been outspoken by one of its commanders, had been shared by some of his subordinates, had entered into their councils, had acted as the dead-weight about their necks in more than one campaign, and, in the opinion of the speaker, had contributed largely to more than one defeat. Have we not the spectacle of a commander dictating from the field, by the midnight lamp, messages of advice upon this subject to Washington, and while those messages were being studied and written, his opponent was preparing against his army a campaign from the toils of which it barely escaped? But, thank God, this sentiment did not appreciably affect the rank and file; and, at the period of which we speak, its baleful element had been largely, if not entirely, eliminated from its councils, and the caps of liberty upon the staffs of our regimental flags stood, for one and all, as no longer the emblems of an idle and groundless dream, but as the symbols of an enunciated and living fact. If we succeeded, it would live the pride and boast of all coming time; if we failed, it would find a grave amid the common wreck.

And now Gen. Lee and his lieutenants, with every external reason for hopefulness of success, sanguine of their own ability, with no shadow of doubt of the constancy of the ragged and dirty, but devoted divisions which they led, knowing that in some instances their soldiers had come to hold in derision the Army of the Potomac, which now alone could bar their progress and wake them and their cause forever from their dream of disunion, had started out to carry the war into the North, and the recognition of their cause in Europe. Says one writer: "The future of America was about to be decided forever."

6

A few days after the vanguard of that invading host had crossed the Rappahannock on the right of our camps at Falmouth, and, in light marching order and with lighter hearts, had sped on well towards the North, Gen. Hooker puts his columns in motion, and, at route step, always the order when a long journey was before it, the Army of the Potomac takes up again its task of protecting its own capital and beating back an invasion. Analyze that task, if you can ; measure its breadth, sound its depth ! Only the plummet of the Almighty can reach the limit. That army comprised a mass—that mass composed of units, every one of those units representing a human heart, a human soul, living, breathing, hoping, loving, to whom the name of home and loved ones was as dear, to many the prattle of whose children was as sweet, and to one and all the desire for life as strong and controlling as are any or all these sentiments to this company to-day. That army, that mass, those units had now become, for the time being, at least, the forlorn hope of its government ; with their bayonets and their bosoms they were to form the last bulwark of defence between the loyal cities of the North, with their industries, their wealth, their homes, their altars and their firesides, and the hitherto victorious arms of Lee.

Do you comprehend the meaning of that task ? In a measure, yes ; but words fail and become impotent in the presence of the facts towards which that oft-defeated army now, with resolute step and determined visage, wends its way. Dante, Shakespeare, Victor Hugo, and Carlyle, have, each in his own way, written of battle scenes ; all have brought their wonderful and varied power of language to bear in reciting the physical transaction ; but which of these has ever depicted the mental phase, or what is felt 'mid the shriek of shrapnel and the whiz of lead ? Go, read them, you soldiers of twenty battles, and see if even these masters of delineation have told all that is experienced 'mid the noise and confusion, the roar of artillery, the crash of small arms, the struggle of death, the hemorrhage of friends, the beseeching look for assistance which you cannot give, and the thousand sickening details of a fight. Men have come out from these scenes without the vestige of a physical bruise, but with mental balance gone, reason dethroned. Physical science teaches that 'tis but a step, but a hair's breath, but a feather's weight, between sane and insane ; but who has ever told what a man may suffer before that weight is changed ?

We left our camps in front of Fredericksburg and the near vicinity of Chancellorsville, without regret, for, saving the graves of comrades tried and true, there was nothing there that did not incite a shudder, and, while we knew instinctively that the campaign upon which we were just entering could not be closed without a fearful struggle, yet the predominant feeling was, anywhere, but there, for the next trial of arms.

The march of the Second Corps, with the soldierly Hancock in command, over long and circuitous routes, sometimes in battle line, sometimes *en masse*, fording rivers and ascending hills, always on the watch as one who peers into the darkness for the foe he knows is there, is without special interest in this narrative, till a point near Taneytown, in northern Maryland, is reached on the 30th of June, at night. We had scarcely resumed our march of the morning, before the sound which we had been for days expecting to make or to hear, was borne upon our ears—that sound, which once heard can never be mistaken, of continuous and increasing artillery fire ; and, although it was miles away, its volume was portentous. Quickly and instinctively the ranks of the sturdy infantry close up, gunners look to their pieces as they have done a score of times before, though, excepting a sponge bucket may need refilling, there is nothing to be done to prepare them for the fray.

At eleven o'clock the hamlet of Taneytown is reached, where the Second Corps is briefly halted, for, at this stage, the plan of battle, which the next few hours was to develop, had not yet had its birth, and in obedience to orders we were not hurried to the front. During this halt we hear of the death of Gen. Reynolds, and we know that one of our ablest and best

has forever sheathed his sword. With this sad news there
also comes the wildest rumors of disaster at the front—of the
First Corps and Buford's Cavalry fairly enveloped by a cloud
of Confederates, before whom they are stubbornly giving
ground.

We knew that splendid First Corps and those equally brave
horsemen, and, if they were giving ground before an enemy
whom they had met, it was evidence conclusive that Gen. Lee
had commenced, if he had not already effected, the concentration of his troops. The probability of this conclusion, and
of the rumors which were rife, was constantly enhanced by
the ever-increasing battle-sound, which tells to the now anxious
minds of both armies that the hour of trial was at hand.

Gen. Meade, with a retinue, gallops not hastily along the
road to where our headquarter flag is seen, and there, with
Hancock, occurs a conference, the import of which all the
world knows. "Go to the front, General, assume command
of the field in my name, bring order, if you can, out of chaos,
if chaos there exists, and report to me promptly the feasibility
of concentration there!" Gen. Hancock enters an ambulance
instead of the saddle, that he may have better opportunity
of studying his maps and plans, while he is driven rapidly
toward the point where danger thickens. Immediately the
weary feet of the Second Corps are moved battle-ward, and
the tired soldier takes heart, for this is the man of whom
Gen. Grant, within a few years, has said that he "never knew
him to make a mistake."

You have already listened to an historical address by Lieut.
Benjamin H. Child, whose triple battle-scars from Bull Run,
from Antietam, and finally, and all but fatally, from this once
shot-torn ground upon which we now stand, so mutely entitle
him to speak in this glad and sad reunion hour ; also to a
brief paper prepared by Capt. Wm. A. Arnold, reciting in
modest words the part his company bore on this eventful
field—Capt. Arnold, whose name we have so proudly inscribed
on this monumental stone, whose cool, intelligent bravery
amid those trying hours lent accuracy to the gunners' aim,

while it imparted strength to the arm and hope to the hearts of his comrades. Would that he were with us to-day to speak for himself, as, in the name of Rhode Island, we apply the finishing touch to her history in that great drama ; to speak not as once at the head of this company he spoke across these fields, carrying death and dismay to countrymen, but rather in the spirit which eighteen centuries ago prompted the great Nazarene, when he taught of "Peace on earth and goodwill to men."

One single thought and I have finished. Said Lord Nelson by signal flag to his fleet at Trafalgar, as clearing their decks for action they bore down on the French and Spanish Armada : " England expects that every man will do his duty." Was that expectation realized? Let her proud and unquestioned supremacy of the seas from that hour to this very day, make answer! Capt. Arnold has told us that every man of his company did his duty on this field. This statement will apply with equal force to the soldiers of every loyal State whose representatives were here. What more did Rhode Island or her sister States ask of their sons ? What more did their government expect of its soldiers ? Were these expectations realized ? Go ask of the thirteen undivided stripes upon yon cemetery flag as it keeps its solemn watch and guard over the bivouac of its dead upon this field—this field which witnessed perhaps one of the grandest exemplifications of American valor it ever beheld ! Go ask of that untarnished field of blue with its star for every State, old and new,—some of whom, though once estranged in their affections, now join with glad and happy hands in the grand confederation of liberty and union ! Go ask of the shackles, mental and physical, which were broken upon this and a hundred other fields! Go ask of the Afric mother, who to-day owns her babe and whose back the lash of arrogant idleness no longer scars! Go ask of the many great questions of state and polity which came up through the regenerating influences of that awful baptism of blood, washed and cleansed forever !

The party then proceeded to the memorial of Battery B,
where the services were continued as follows :

ADDRESS BY MR. JOHN DELEVAN,

Who Served as a Private in Battery B, at the Battle of Gettysburg.

*Mr. Chairman, Ladies and Gentlemen, and my old Comrades
of the War : -*

I feel more like sitting down and bowing my head and let-
ting memory take its sway at this time and place, than in at-
tempting to speak. Although the surroundings and the face
of the country have a familiar look, still there seems to be
something missing, which memory all the while is trying to
fill with regiments, brigades, divisions, batteries, and all the
paraphernalia of the grand old Army of the Potomac engaged
in desperate battle. I find it very difficult to realize the present while the recollections of the past crowd themselves in
serried columns, as it were, on the mind. At the first glance
backward it seems hardly possible that twenty-three years and
upwards have been added to our lives since our first visit to
this spot, when we marched up in column across those fields
to take our position in line and share with the old Second
Corps the destinies of battle, and also to secure a spot for this
monument. It is but natural that a small company like ours,
continually in the face of danger, should become intimately
acquainted with one another and as strongly attached as one
family under one roof, for we had shared alike together the
dangers and excitement of battle and skirmish, the suffering
of hunger and thirst, the fatigues of the long and tedious
march by day and by night, in sunshine and rain, the longing
for home and loved ones, and often in the lone hours of night,
when on post, we would meet at the end of our beats and
converse in low tones of our homes, and tell to one another
our plans and what we intended to do if we lived to arrive
safe at home. Many of them never lived to enjoy the realiza
tion of their cherished plans and desires, but have passed

hence on this and other fields, or from lingering disease, or from wounds received. I feel that we, the survivors, have much to be thankful for, that we have been spared from the sad casualties of war, and our hearts should be filled with gratitude to a kind Providence which has guided our marches by day and by night, and permitted us to gather here after so many years. As I stand on this sacred spot, I cannot help comparing the occasion of this visit with that of our first visit so many years ago. We have a duty to perform to-day ; we had a duty to perform then ; but what a vast difference in these duties ! To-day we are here to dedicate the monuments contributed by the State of Rhode Island in grateful recognition of our services in this desperate battle. Well might Rhode Island be proud of her soldiers, for they fought side by side with the best troops of other States, and have met in battle array the choicest troops of the Confederacy, and on no field, under no circumstances, has the honor of Rhode Island suffered at their hands, especially her artillery. We are here to-day to dedicate this monument, sacred to the memory of our unfortunate and revered comrades who fell at this place, dying in the full vigor of manhood. Death, under the most favorable circumstances, is terrible to contemplate ; but to the soldier on the field of carnage—torn, mangled, bleeding, dying in the full vigor of manhood and health, with all the bright prospects of future glory blotted out forever ! O, how my heart throbbed in agony as I saw them fall on this field !— comrades whom I had associated with for nearly two years, sharing with them the dangers of other fields, sharing together our scanty rations, drinking from the same canteen, and gathered around the camp-fire they told me their lives, their hopes, read to me their loving letters from home. Cruel, cruel war ! I feel that we are here to-day to dedicate this monument to the memory of Battery B, the pride of our hearts, and the grandest, choicest recollections of our lives.

Battery B was mustered in at Providence, Aug. 13th, 1861, for the period of three years, and proceeded immediately to Washington, where we went into quarters at Camp Sprague,

and received our guns and horses. Then we marched to
Poolesville, Md., near where we had our first fight, the disastrous battle of Ball's Bluff, and lost one gun and nearly a
whole gun detachment. In the spring of '62 we took part in
the capture of Winchester under Gen. Banks, after which we
proceeded to Washington, where the battery joined the forces
of Gen. McClellan, and took a very active part in the siege of
Yorktown and the rest of the campaign. Then came South
Mountain, Antietam, first and second Fredericksburg. In the
first battle of Fredericksburg we were ordered into what we
termed a forlorn hope. I will make a short mention of it
here. It was the 13th day of December, the day of the hard
fighting. We were in reserve until near night, when we were
ordered to report to Gen. Howard, who commanded a division
of the Second Corps. We moved to the front, to the edge of
the city, and found Gen. Howard watching the battle. I
heard him tell our captain that he was about to order a charge
on the enemy's works, and it was necessary for a smooth-bore
battery to go up first and to fire rapidly, not stop to cut fire,
but to create a cloud of smoke to hide the troops and to give
them courage. And then he said : " Capt. Hazard, I do not
expect you to come out—with your guns, at least." The
battery dashed in. Our loss was heavy for the length of time
we were engaged. The charge was repulsed. The battery
took a part in the second battle of Fredericksburg, and had
the pleasure of assisting in the capture of the heights. At
this battle the section to which I belonged fought a duel with
a section of the famous Confederate Washington Artillery.

One day in June we received orders to pack up and be
ready to move at night, but not to strike tents till dark, as
we were camped in sight of the enemy across the river.
When it became dark our tents were struck, and then commenced our march for Gettysburg. But we were not then
aware of our destination. We marched nearly all night,
forming lines of battle so as to be prepared to receive the
enemy if they should attempt to follow. The next day was
very hot, and it told on us, as we had had no sleep the night

before, and we had been camping with shades over us. In
the afternoon the road was strewn with the dead and dying
from the effects of the sun. Our corps had a skirmish at
Thoroughfare Gap on our way, after which we crossed the
Potomac into Maryland, near Leesburg, in the vicinity of our
first battle, Ball's Bluff. On we went through Poolesville into
Pennsylvania. We now began to understand the intent of
the enemy, and our greatest anxiety was,—Would we be in
time? I remember the anxious look of the residents along
our route in Pennsylvania, as they came running to the road-
side—men, women, and children. After noon on July 1st,
we heard distant firing of artillery, and, as we reached the
top of a hill, we saw away in the distance the smoke of battle.
Then we knew the Army of the Potomac was in time. At
dark we arrived near the field. The Second Corps threw
themselves down to rest and sleep. Poor, weary men! the
next night many of them will sleep the eternal sleep. The
next morning we started for the front line. As we marched
across those fields, there were columns at the right of us, and
columns at the left of us. One thing, in particular, I observed, that on other similar occasions there would be more
or less cheering and other demonstrations of enthusiasm, but
on this occasion, everyone appeared dumb, silent, stern. It
might have been from the effects of their long and fatiguing
march, but to me it seemed that they realized the great im-
portance of the issues at stake in the coming battle. Behind
us were our homes and all we held dear ; above us, the starry
flag, which, next to Heaven, we most revered ; in front of us,
our old adversary, the gallant Army of Northern Virginia,
with its skillful leader, and its bravest and most experienced
corps commanders, flushed with the knowledge of previous
victories, and joyous in expectations of present success. Between the two armies, on an open field and no favors, nearly
equal in numbers, there was about to take place a struggle of
giants, on the issue of which hung the destiny of this continent. Well might the soldier of the Army of the Potomac
be silent and thoughtful.

The battery occupied three positions on this field ; first, in the morning, at our left and front, where you see those shocks of corn, but we were not engaged there, but moved to the right, and taking position on that small ridge in front of the line of battle and forming a spur from the main line, facing at right oblique, but firing left oblique—a very awkward position, especially for the left of the battery, as when our skirmishers were drawn in, which was the case, our left flank would be in the air. As we went into position here, we observed the chimneys, and roofs, and steeples of a village at our right and front. We asked what town it was, and soon word was passed,—Gettysburg ! We had never heard of such a place before, but, soon, thousands of hearts, North and South, would throb in anguish at the mention of Gettysburg.

I will relate some of the incidents of our share of the second day's battle, as I saw it. I was gunner of the left gun, the farthest from the main line. The sergeant of our gun observed, as he dismounted, that he hoped this would be the wickedest old fight the battery was ever in. He had his wish gratified, and it was the sergeant's last fight in Battery B. The ground had recently been plowed, and made a good position for our guns in action, as they could not recoil. The sun shone hot, and there was no shade. For a long time we stood or reclined around our guns, waiting the opening of the Book of Fate. The enemy's sharpshooters crawled up in our front, and made targets of us. One of them closed one of his eyes on me, and the bullet passed between my arm and body. Near four o'clock there was a movement at our left, which caused us to spring to our feet. The Third Corps was moving to the front. As our position was, we had to face partly to the rear to see them. It was one of the grandest sights I ever witnessed. They did not move in line of battle, but in a solid mass. The sun shone on bright guns, and glistening bayonets ; and the waving colors, and their steady, compact movements made a picture of dazzling beauty. We were surprised at this movement, for we did not expect to be the attacking party. The boys said to one another,—They cannot go far in that direction before they will strike a snag. Soon from the edge of the woods in their front came puffs of smoke, then, bang! bang! Soon there was a commotion in the Third Corps, and in a few moments they were hotly engaged. From where we stood we could look over them, and see the enemy emerge from the woods, and they came on gallantly, firing as they came. We could see them close in on the left flank of the Third Corps. We saw Gen. Meade and staff dashing out to them, and saw the enemy fire on him from the left. Then we knew it was all day with the Third. Soon a regiment broke, then a brigade, then a division; then it appeared that the whole corps was in full retreat, coming back. But what a difference from their going out! The disaster to the Third Corps filled us with dismay and anxiety, as we did not know what the result would be, for the enemy were following them sharply, and where would the Third stop? I heard some of the boys exclaim, "Whipped again!" and it did look shaky. A part of our corps (the Second) had already been sent to their assistance. There has been much discussion, of late, in regard to the disaster to the Third Corps, and to whom the blame, if any, should be attached. It is not my purpose to quote anybody else's opinion, but to give my own from the evidence of my own eyes. It was, and is, my opinion, that the disastrous result of the move proved it to have been a mistake, and the blame must necessarily be attached to the person who ordered it, whether it was the general commanding, or the corporal of the guard. Surely, there should be no blame attached to the men in the ranks, for they made no mistakes, and disobeyed no orders; they did the best they could, for the old Third was a fighting corps. The best troops that ever formed a line could not have withstood that front and flank attack. But there was one fortunate circumstance, for, if some officer did blunder, the men in the ranks knew enough to retreat when badly beaten, as, if they had staid, they would have been annihilated, and the Army of the Potomac could not afford to lose so many good fighters at so critical a time.

Our attention was suddenly called from the Third Corps by the rapid discharge of artillery on our right. We about-faced and saw at our front, away off near the woods, a Confederate battle-flag apparently lifting itself up out of the ground, and then two rows of heads, and then the shoulders of a long line of battle. As yet we had made no move or preparation, but stood gazing at them in silence, and well we might, for they were a grand object to behold. At first we saw them as they came up the slope, now their heads, next their shoulders and bodies, in a long circling line. There was something terribly suggestive in their steady advance, denoting that their visit to us was not of pleasure, but purely of business. I suggested to the sergeant that we had better prepare for business, as the Johnnies were coming for us. The sergeant said, " No, they are our men coming in." At that movement a sheet of smoke rolled up from them, then a crackling of their rifles, and the dirt flew among us. I asked the sergeant if he didn't think our men were careless with their guns. Immediately we heard our commanding officer shout to us to open on them at once ; " They are the enemy!" Instantly the whole machinery of the battery was set in motion. A quick opening of ammunition chests, a running of powder-monkeys, a whirling of sponge staffs—" Ready, fire !"—and, out from the front of Battery B, leaped jetting flames : the sulphurous smoke enveloped the cannoneers as a cloud of dirt spurted up among the enemy from our shots, but it made no impression on them. We were using fixed ammunition, firing about five times per minute from each gun. We had at first to fire at an elevation, but, as they advanced, we kept depressing our pieces till at a point-blank. Then the enemy's fire was terrible. The air around us appeared alive with lead. Once I glanced up along the line, while in the fiercest of the fight, and pride took the place of fear. It was a sad but glorious sight to see how splendidly the boys were handling the guns. Our smoke was rolling back over the main line. There seemed to be a constant jetting of flame from the front of the battery. At every limber some of the horses were down, flouncing in the

agonies of death, but the guns were jumping and roaring, not
appearing to miss a cog. Every one of the boys seemed to
be earning his thirteen dollars per month. The enemy were
now piling over the two fences at the road in our front; the few
men who were on our left were running past us, and our left
flank was now in the air with no support. Our fire was very
destructive to the enemy. I could see, at every discharge of
one of our guns, a vacant space appear in the enemy's ranks,
but they would immediately close up, so it was like dropping
a stone into water. But on they came, with their slouch hats
pulled over their eyes, bringing their guns to the shoulder and
firing. We could see their hands go up and down as they
loaded as they advanced. They were now sweeping around
on our left, and at this moment two men were shot at our
gun, a powder-monkey and the sergeant. The latter and I
were disputing about the management of the gun, when the
shot struck him. We now began to realize that we were in a
critical place, and should have been ordered back when the
troops fell back. If we staid much longer, we would all be
killed or taken prisoners. We were pleased when we heard
the command to limber to the rear. But now came the
greatest difficulty, to get our gun off, as the enemy were most
on to us. We had to cease firing to hitch on to the gun.
Those who have been in close quarters in a battery can realize
what an ordeal it is for the drivers to mount in the saddle
right in the face of the enemy. I know that two men at this
time were spilled out of one saddle by the enemy in succession, one killed, the other wounded. As the order to limber
up was given, I shouted to the drivers, who had already
mounted, to advance. I was standing beside the trail looking
over my shoulder to see if we had time. There were but a few
yards between the gun and the enemy. But the drivers would
not come, for all I could do or say. They dashed up to the right
and hitched on to the next gun, and away. The cannoneers,
who were standing at the gun, now became discouraged and
ran for the rear, leaving me and the gun. I could not blame
them, for there was now no prospect of saving the gun. A

despair seized me, and I threw myself down beside the gun
to share its fate. Those drivers told me, afterwards, that the
reason they would not come to the gun was that the enemy
were as close to the gun as they were, which was about eleven
yards. But the gun was saved for all that. I had but just
thrown myself down when I heard a rattling of chains.
Looking up, I saw a limber coming at a dashing gait from the
wall. Our caissons were in rear of the main line, and as soon
as the limbers at the pieces became nearly exhausted, those
of the caissons would take their places. This proved to be
one sent to our piece, not knowing that we were ordered out.
Some of the detachment were returning with it. The limber,
with its six horses on full run, created a cloud of dust in the
plowed ground, and had the appearance of a charge. I sprang
up and glanced at the enemy to see if we would have time to
limber the gun. I observed that the rebs had come to a halt,
apparently fixing bayonets, which gave us time, and caused
them the loss of the gun. All of this did not occupy more
than one minute. I remember, as the limber dashed up, there
were three of the Fifteenth Massachusetts boys who had been
fighting on our left and front, but the regiment had retreated.
The three men came running to us, saying, "For God's sake,
get this gun out of here, quick!" One of them dropped his
gun and helped to lift the trail. The other two faced the
enemy, and discharged their guns in their faces. The gun
was limbered, the drivers lashed and spurred their horses,
and away went the gun through the wall fifty yards away. I
had become completely exhausted. I tried to catch hold of
the sight of the gun to pull me along, but I missed it and fell
on my face. The enemy had discovered their mistake and
were after us. As I reached about half-way to the wall, I
saw the gun go through. The Sixty-Ninth had been impa-
tiently waiting for us to get out of the way, so they could
have a hand at the rebs. With feelings of despair, I saw
them thrust the muzzles of their guns across the wall. As I
looked at the row of dark muzzles pointing down on me, it
was no pleasant sight. Then came a sheet of flame and

smoke ; and whiz! came their bullets. Here the poor fellow
of the Fifteenth Massachusetts, who helped at the trail, fell
dead at my side. I then thought my days on earth were
numbered. It seemed to me I should die a dozen deaths before I could reach the wall. I have heard it said that, when
a person faces certain death, the whole of his past life comes
instantly before his eyes. I believe it to be a fact, for on this
occasion I thought I was as good as dead, and I am not
ashamed to say that the home of my childhood and the dear
friends of my youth came before my vision, and to me, just
emerging from boyhood to young manhood, life was precious,
and the thoughts of death terrible. I had but little fear of
future judgment, for I believed that my Creator would have
more mercy on this poor, weary young soldier, who had tried
his best to do his duty this day, than that screeching, yelling
mob at my heels. In front of the wall was a hole about ten
yards across and reaching within two yards of the wall, and
about four feet deep in the middle, but tapering up to the
edge. I was not aware of this place, and as I came to it I
was blinded by the smoke of the Sixty-Ninth, their fire being
hot in my face. I fell into this hole, and I lay where I fell.
I raised my head to see what station it was, and I discovered
a man of my detachment reclining on the other side under the
fire of the Sixty-Ninth. As he saw me he smiled ; I suppose,
at my coming in, for I did not stand on the order of my coming, but I just came. The enemy halted here and lay down,
some of them at the edge of the hole, and fired across. Here
the two lines were about twelve yards apart, so near that they
quarrelled as they fought. Every time the Sixty-Ninth fired,
they accompanied it with a shout. The rebs screamed back.
I felt confident that the rebs would be defeated, as I knew
that the Sixty-Ninth would not give in, for they told us when
we took our position that they would protect us while they had
a man left, and gallantly they redeemed their promise. There
were other troops engaged, but the Sixty-Ninth were our special support. The survivors of Battery B will always carry
in their hearts a grateful remembrance of the brave Irish

Sixty-Ninth Pennsylvania. I made up my mind while lying there, that, as soon as the rebs were defeated, I would make a dash for the wall, for there were two rebs firing across me, and they could touch me with their guns. Suddenly the enemy ceased firing. I jumped up to make a dive for the wall, but, like Lot's wife, I looked back. Those two rebs had got up to run. As they did so, I heard two voices say from the wall, " Come in, you sons of ——!" I glanced quickly at the wall, and there stood two of the Sixty-Ninth with their guns at their shoulders, with fingers on the triggers, their eyes glancing along the barrels. At first I thought they had mistaken me, but I was so close to them I could see one of them was aiming by my right shoulder, the other by my left. They had got the drop on those two rebs, who threw their guns down as if they were hot. We three came over the wall together. I found my gun at the rear of the Sixty-Ninth. They had given me up for dead, and Billy Jones was acting as gunner in my stead. Poor Billy! he was killed the next day. This ended this day's fight.

It was now evening. I remember it was a very pleasant evening overhead, the moon was shining bright. But it was a sickening sight under foot—dead and wounded everywhere. There was a detail made from our men to go down on our position to take care of any dead, and to secure the harnesses of our dead horses. I went with them. I shall never forget the sight. The ground where we fought, and in front, was covered with dead. We could tell where our guns stood, by the piles of dead horses. I forgot to state that the Sixty-Ninth charged after the enemy as I came over the wall. They captured several hundred of them, and as they were taking them to the rear, they passed through our battery. The rebs recognized us, and saluted us with curses loud and deep. They swore that if they ever got another chance at us, they would cut our hearts out, and there would not be a grease spot left of our battery. We did not reply to them, for we knew that Battery B had stung them, and they were smarting from its effects. As our loss in men and horses had been severe, and our rations had given out the day before, we expected to be relieved, as we knew there were batteries in the rear that had not fired a shot ; but, instead of relief, two of our guns were sent to the rear so as to consolidate the men on the other four. Instead of rations, ammunition was sent to us. That night we slept the sleep of the tired and hungry.

The morning of July 3d found the battery on the line of artillery, on the left of Cushing's Battery A, of the Fourth Regulars, in which Lieut. Milne, of our battery, was serving for the time being, having been mortally wounded. Here we remained all the forenoon, waiting as we did the day before, not knowing what was in store for us. And well it was that we did not know. The enemy kept quiet in our front, except, now and then, from different points along their lines, would come a shot. They were, unknown to us, placing all their artillery in position, and, as a battery came in, it would fire a shot to get the range. I would say, it was about one o'clock when they opened the "gates of hell," so to speak. At that time I was sleeping in the shade of a caisson, and was awakened by an awful crash. I sprang up. The ground was trembling, shells bursting over and among us. Some of their shots were ploughing lengthways of the battery, and from every direction but the rear. I cannot, nor shall not, attempt to describe the horrors of that time. I remember, at first, I was completely bewildered. Waking from a sound sleep, I ran to the left of the battery to find my gun, forgetting, in my excitement, that it was one of the two that had been sent to the rear. At that instant I was struck on the left shoulder by a piece of shell, which had the effect of waking me up. I shall never forget the terrible effect of that artillery fire. There were horses with their inwards dragging on the ground. In rear of us was a regiment lying on the ground, with their guns stuck in the ground by the bayonets. I saw those guns flying in the air like ten-pins, and I saw men scooped up in the air by the plunging shots. I went to what is now known

8

as the Gettysburg gun,* where I found Billy Jones cutting
fuses, and I assisted him. We were firing very fast. We
expended the ammunition at that limber, and then we went
to the gun and stood near the trail conversing. Bob Wilkin-
son, who was handling the sponge-staff, had become exhausted,
and was calling for relief. Billy said, "I will spell Bob," and
went to his relief. I saw that the next gun was minus a
gunner, and, as that was my rank, I went to it. Sergeant
Horton was at the trail. I had been there but a few minutes
when there was a crash, and Horton exclaimed, "My God!
there goes two of our men!" I gave one look, and became
faint and sick for a moment. Such a sight I never want to
see again. There sat Gardiner, faced to the rear, with the
side of his body next to me torn away, his shoulder and arm
hanging in shreds, his vitals exposed, as he sat dazed. The
sergeant of the gun ran to him to hear his dying words.
Gardiner, who was Number Two, had just inserted the charge
as the enemy's shell came at rather left oblique, striking him
in the side, and on the side of the face of the muzzle of the
gun, and exploded. The explosion blew Jones several yards
to the front, the sponge staff farther on, completely beheading
him. Jones had just sponged the piece, and was at a reverse,
waiting for Gardiner to insert the charge. The shell, the part
of it as it exploded that did not cover the muzzle of the gun,
passed under it, carrying away a part of the axle. I said I
felt faint when I saw the effects of that cruel shot. Those
two men I was very intimate with. While the battery
was organizing at Providence, Jones and I boarded at the
same house, and we became very intimate, and during
the war, up to this battle, we were warm friends. He had
served in the navy, and he gave me my first experience in
the use of the sabre, with which he was very handy. He

* This gun was captured by the enemy the night before, the horses on it having been
killed just before it arrived at the wall. The gallant Sixty-Ninth and the enemy fought
desperately for its possession, but the Irishmen wrenched it from the rebels' grasp. The
gunner of this gun, I am told, did not desert the gun, but lay on the ground beside it while
the desperate struggle took place. I did not witness the struggle for the gun, although I
was but a few yards to the right, for I was at that time very busy holding that hole.

was a splendid artilleryman, and one of the best shots in the battery. I remember, the night of our departure from Providence on the boat train, he and I occupied the same seat, and as we were hurrying along to our new existence, we sat a long time in silence. At last, Billy turned to me and said, "Johnny, this is the going, but what will the returning be?" Poor Billy! how I missed him in the weary months that followed! Gardiner came to us as a recruit; I do not remember at what period, but he had been with us quite a long time. He was rather peculiar, but a good, quiet, steady man, performing his duty conscientiously, very pious, his Bible being his constant companion—a man who feared God, and tried to live up to, and practice his belief, in all the excitement and temptations of the soldier's life. I would often talk of his family, whom he was proud of and had the greatest affection for. He carried a small book besides his Bible, and I observed that he used it to press flowers in, which did not grow at home; and when he wrote to his wife, which was very often, he would send them to her. Sergeant Straight, of the gun on which he was killed, was a chum of his, and they tented together. I heard that they had promised one another, that if either was killed or wounded, the survivor would, if possible, come to the fallen one's side. It was Sergeant Straight that I saw run to the side of Gardiner to hear his dying words. I could see Gardiner's lips move, as if speaking, but I could not hear what he said, except the last words, which I heard very distinctly; they were, "Glory halleluia!" After the battle the sergeant told me the rest of the sentence. Gardiner told him to take his book and Bible, which were in the side of his blouse that was not shot away, and send them to his wife, and tell her that he died happy; then he shouted the words which I heard. That was the death of the christian soldier Gardiner. One of the men ran and procured an axe and tried to drive the shell down into the gun in order to fire it, as the powder was attached to the shell, but to no purpose. Another shell exploded at the gun, and mortally wounded No. Four, John Green. As this piece was now useless, we had but three

left, and no ammunition. Orders came to retire. The battery
had difficulty to find horses enough to haul off the guns and
caissons. Some had three, some more. One gun, in retiring
from the field, was swept clean of horses by a shell, and had
to be left till the battery got off the field; and when they came
back for it, it was not to be found. Some other battery,
which had lost a gun, took it. As our officers had neglected
to keep the numbers of the guns, it was never found. I understood that our officers had to pay for it, but the money
was afterwards refunded. Just before the battery retired, I
was crippled, so that I could not go at that time, but I knew
that I would be able to go soon. As I lay on the ground,
watching the relief batteries going into position, suddenly I
saw a regiment, which had been lying on the ground near us,
spring up and grasp their guns, which were sticking in the
ground by the bayonets, and run to the front. I gave one
glance in that direction. That one glance was enough for
me,—the Johnnies were charging. Thinking there was no
call for me here, as the battery was away, and recollecting
how I got mixed up in the infantry fight the night before, I
just put after the battery. But, before I got out of hearing,
I heard the hearty cheering of our men, and I knew the field
was won.

I do not remember exactly the number of men we lost
in the two days' fight. I know our loss in killed was eight
men, not including Lieut. Milne, who was killed, or mortally wounded, in Battery A, of the 4th United States. His
death was a loss to us, and a sad loss. One man was taken
prisoner. I think about thirty were wounded, among which
was 1st Lieut. T. Fred. Brown, commanding the battery. Our
captain, John G. Hazard, was chief of artillery of the corps.
Our loss in horses was very great. One gun was disabled, one
stolen. The battery was condemned as unfit for duty. The
surviving men and horses were placed in Battery A, which
battery had fought gallantly and suffered severely. We were
with them two or three months. Then we received four guns,
and Battery B was itself again. I shall always remember

with gratitude, the kind and considerate treatment of the officers and men of Battery A towards us poor homeless men of Battery B, while we were with them.

In conclusion, I wish to thank the ladies and gentlemen who have been to the trouble and expense of accompanying us here, and I bid them welcome to this sacred and historic spot, the high-water mark of the great rebellion.

PRESENTATION ADDRESS BY MR. D. COIT TAYLOR, WHO SERVED AS AN ARTIFICER IN BATTERY B.

Mr. Krauth :—And now it becomes my pleasant duty, as a representative of the State and of the battery, to place in your keeping this granite tablet. And may its summit point up to Heaven for generations, its base be watered by the dews of the returning seasons, the sun light up its sides with its golden rays, and the tears of angels keep ever green this hallowed spot, made sacred by the blood of heroes of a common and now united country.

PRESENTATION ADDRESS BY LIEUT. BENJ. H. CHILD, OF BATTERY A.

Mr. Secretary :—I have the pleasure of presenting to the Gettysburg Battlefield Memorial Association, through you, this beautiful granite memorial of Battery A, First Rhode Island Light Artillery, for its perpetual care and protection, knowing, as we do, that it is placed in good and faithful hands, and that it will be well done.

RESPONSE BY SECRETARY KRAUTH.

Mr. Chairman, Veterans of Batteries A and B, Ladies and Gentlemen :—I can add nothing to what I have already said at the memorial of the Second Rhode Island, as to the purposes and desires of the Association I represent, to carefully guard these monuments. The ground on which we stand is hallowed and sacred, if there be any ground on the continent

that is so. It was here that the Confederate chieftain made
the last attempt on Northern soil to restore the waning fortunes of his cause. I think that these men of Rhode Island
should esteem it a great good fortune to have been on this
spot at that time, as it was their guns, double-shotted, which
could repel the enemy from this field. It is especially fitting
that Rhode Island should have monuments on this field, since
that ancient commonwealth was the first organized government in the world to establish impartial religious toleration.
In conclusion, I assure you that our Association will preserve
these monuments, and all others upon this field, confided to
us, from the hand of the spoiler, and that nothing but the
corroding finger of time shall ever molest or disturb them.

Benediction by Chaplain Webb.

The party then returned by train to the station at Gettysburg.

Wednesday afternoon and Thursday morning, under the
guidance of Col. John B. Bachelder, Superintendent of Tablets
and Legends of the Gettysburg Battlefield Memorial Association, and Government Historian of the Battle of Gettysburg,
who met the excursion at Harrisburg and accompanied it to
its destination, the party visited the various points of interest
on the battlefield, the graphic description of Col. Bachelder
adding greatly to their satisfaction.

After dinner, at the Eagle Hotel, on Thursday, that being
the last meal before starting for home, it was unanimously

Voted, That the Rhode Island Excursion to Gettysburg, thor-
oughly appreciating the kindly courtesy of Col. Bachelder in accompanying it to its destination, and how much his genial and
instructive presence has contributed to the enjoyment of the occasion, hereby extend to him its most grateful acknowledgment and
warmest thanks.

At the same time, a vote gratefully recognizing the services of the Manager, and Excursion Committee, was likewise passed. In this connection, mention should be made of the following gentlemen, to whose courteous attentions the Excursion was under many obligations, viz.: Osmund H. Briggs, General Passenger Agent, New York, Providence and Boston R. R. Co.; Capt. John H. Markley, Travelling Passenger Agent, Pennsylvania R. R. Co.; John B. Bagley, General Travelling Agent, Cumberland Valley R. R. Co.; William H. Woodward, Superintendent, Harrisburg and Gettysburg R. R. Co.; Henry Yingling, Proprietor, and Rufus E. Culp, Chief Clerk, Eagle Hotel, Gettysburg; Simon J. Diller, Proprietor, McClellan House, Gettysburg; and John M. Krauth, David Buehler, Col. Charles H. Buehler, John L. Schick, and William D. Holtzworth, Local Members of the Board of Trustees of the Gettysburg Battlefield Memorial Association.

Thursday afternoon came the departure from Gettysburg, either directly for home or via such points of interest as individual desire dictated.

At a meeting of the Excursion Committee, held shortly after the return, the Chairman was appointed a committee to procure and present to Col. John B. Bachelder, and to the Manager, Gen. E. H. Rhodes, suitable testimonials of the Excursion's appreciation of their services, and accordingly a massive bronze thermometer and a silver-plated coffee urn, suitably inscribed, were forwarded to the respective parties. The chairman, Gen. Horatio Rogers, was appointed a committee to prepare a record of the excursion, and to supervise its publication.

Thus ended one of the pleasantest and most successful excursions that ever left Rhode Island.